eVANGELIUM

A Multimedia Course in the Catholic Faith
Based on the *Catechism of the Catholic Church*

PRESENTER'S GUIDE

A step by step guide to presenting each session of the
EVANGELIUM course to classes and small groups

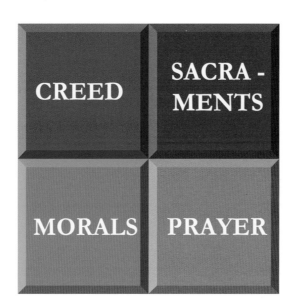

CREED

SACRA-
MENTS

MORALS

PRAYER

Fr. Marcus Holden M.A. (Oxon.), S.T.L.

Archdiocese of Southwark

Fr. Andrew Pinsent M.A. (Oxon.), D.Phil., S.T.B., Ph.L.

Diocese of Arundel and Brighton

Catholic Truth Society

Nihil obstat: Father Anton Cowan, Censor. *Imprimatur:* Rt. Rev. Alan Hopes,V.G., Auxiliary Bishop in Westminster, Westminster, 3rd July 2006, Feast of St. Thomas, Apostle. The *Nihil obstat* and *Imprimatur* are a declaration that a book or pamphlet is considered to be free from doctrinal or moral error. It is not implied that those who have granted the *Nihil obstat* and *Imprimatur* agree with the contents, opinions or statements expressed.

Acknowledgements

The authors extend their thanks to the Catholic Truth Society, especially the members of the editorial board and staff who encouraged the development of EVANGELIUM from a catechetical course delivered at the Venerable English College in Rome to a final published product: Bishop Paul Hendricks, Mr Fergal Martin, Fr Peter Edwards, Ms Glynn Johnson, Mr Pierpaolo Finaldi, Mr Richard Brown and Mr Stephen Campbell. They also thank the professors of the Pontifical Gregorian University, especially Fr Kevin Flannery S.J., Emeritus Dean of Philosophy, and Fr Joseph Carola S.J., Professor of Patristic Theology, for their detailed reviews of the theological and philosophical content. Similarly, they express their gratitude to Rev. Michel Remery, Rev. Bruno Witchalls, Rev. John Flynn, Mr Christopher Miller, Mr Neil Brett, Mr James Mackay, Mr David Charters and the members of the 'Bellarmine Project' for their reviews and suggestions. The authors also acknowledge all those who have encouraged and co-operated in a multitude of ways, including Revv. Tim Finigan, Mark Vickers, Nicholas Schofield, Richard Whinder, Richard Biggerstaff and Stephen Langridge. The authors also thank their parents, John and Irene Holden and Charles and Teresa Pinsent, for their on-going moral support, prayers and advice.

ISBN: 1 86082 394 7 (CTS Code EV2)

Other Evangelium Resources
Evangelium Participant's Book, ISBN 1 86082 393 9; CTS Code EV1; Published 2006
Evangelium CDRom, CTS Code EV3; Published 2006

Contents

PRESENTER'S GUIDE

Presenter's Introduction

Aim of EVANGELIUM

The EVANGELIUM multimedia catechetical course teaches the essentials of Catholic faith and life in a straightforward, precise and attractive manner. It is based on the *Catechism of the Catholic Church* and it is structured in the same fourfold way: Creed, Sacraments, Morals and Prayer.

There are twenty-five modular teaching sessions of about 1 hour 10 minutes duration each.

Creed	Sacraments	Morals	Prayer
10 Sessions	5 Sessions	5 Sessions	5 Sessions

Who is EVANGELIUM for?

EVANGELIUM is for all those who wish to deepen their knowledge of the Catholic Faith, whether or not they are practising members of the Church.

The course materials are intended principally for those participating in the *Rite of Christian Initiation for Adults* (RCIA) or other adult catechetical programmes. They can also be used for Confirmation preparation, youth catechesis, marriage preparation and self-instruction. They have been designed for classes, small groups and individual use.

The aim of this Presenter's Guide

The principal aim of this *Presenter's Guide* is to assist those who are introducing the course presentations to classes or small groups. It may also assist those who are using the course materials to teach themselves.

The *Presenter's Guide* should be used in conjunction with the following:

EVANGELIUM CD	A self-starting CD with twenty-five PowerPoint Viewer© presentations, one for each teaching session.
Participant's Book	A description of the teaching content of the course. This is in the form of a two page summary of each session for each participant.

Who can present an EVANGELIUM course?

Anyone can present an EVANGELIUM course by following the simple instructions in this *Presenter's Guide*. Although background knowledge of the Catholic Faith would be helpful in explaining certain points, it is not necessary for the presenter to be a theological expert on any of the matters covered in the course. The task of the presenter is to facilitate, that is, to make it easy for participants to find the materials they need.

How do I get started quickly?

The quickest way to get started with EVANGELIUM is to read a few pages from the *Participant's Book* and look at one or two presentations on the CD. Each of the twenty-five sessions of the course has the same basic structure, so it is very easy to learn to use the whole course from just a small sample of the material.

How do I plan and present an EVANGELIUM course?

GUIDELINES FOR GENERAL COURSE PREPARATION

- Obtain the following:
  - One copy of the EVANGELIUM CD and one copy of the *Presenter's Guide*.
  - One copy of the *Participant's Book* for <u>each</u> participant and one for the presenter.
  - A personal computer (PC) running one of the following operating systems: Windows XP; Windows Server 2003; Windows ME; Windows 2000 Service Pack 3; Windows 98 Second Edition.
  - A PC projector or a large PC monitor for wide-angle viewing. The ideal arrangement is to have a PC projector to project the images from the PC onto a large wall or screen.
  - A copy of the Bible (ideally, the Revised Standard Version Catholic Edition) and the *Catechism of the Catholic Church* at every session. A copy of the *Compendium of the Cathechism* would also be helpful.
- Plan the order in which the sessions will be taught. Since each session can stand alone it can be taught (i) by itself; (ii) as part of a short course with a few other sessions; or (iii) in a complete twenty-five session programme. Pages 53 and 54 of this book give two possible sequences.

GUIDELINES FOR SESSION PREPARATION

- Read through the relevant two pages of the *Participant's Book* and run through the presentation on the CD at least once to become familiar with the teaching content of the session.
- Read through the relevant two pages of this *Presenter's Guide*. It is recommended to:
  - Read the relevant sections of the *Catechism* and *Compendium* listed in the preparation box.
  - Prepare short statements of introduction, summary and conclusion for the session (the *Presenter's Guide* offers suggestions for all of these).
  - Read through the brief descriptions of the artwork for extra information on the meaning of the pictures. Refer to the appendix of the *Presenter's Guide* for the artists' background.
  - Select from the CD presentation one or more of the optional summary activities which conclude both parts of the session to reinforce the learning points.
  - Select one or more of the follow-up activities to be completed by participants to reinforce the learning points after the session.

GUIDELINES FOR PRESENTING A SESSION

- Load the CD before the start of the session:
  - Put the CD into the CD drive on your PC. After a few moments, typically about 20 seconds on a standard PC, the EVANGELIUM main screen should appear automatically.
  - If the CD does not start automatically, find the PPTVIEW.EXE on the CD manually and double click to run the program. Then, within the opening menu, select EVANGELIUM 2006 to start.
- Begin the session with a prayer. The prayer of St Thomas Aquinas is offered on page ix as a model.
- Introduce the session.
- Lead the class through the sequence of PowerPoint[©] slides.

  It is acceptable to simply read out the text from the slides. However, as the eye reads faster than the ear can hear, a presenter can add greater value either: (i) by drawing attention to one key point; or (ii) by making a brief link to some other course point or personal experience.

- Summarise each part of the session with a brief statement of what has been learnt and one or more of the activities found on the CD.
- Conclude the whole session with a closing statement and a prayer. You may also wish to invite the participants to complete one or more follow-up activities themselves to reinforce the learning points of the session. Examples of all of these are provided in the pages of this *Presenter's Guide*.

How do I select an EVANGELIUM presentation from the CD?

The screen in the top left hand corner of the table below should appear when the CD is started. Click on a subject area and then a particular presentation button to start that presentation.

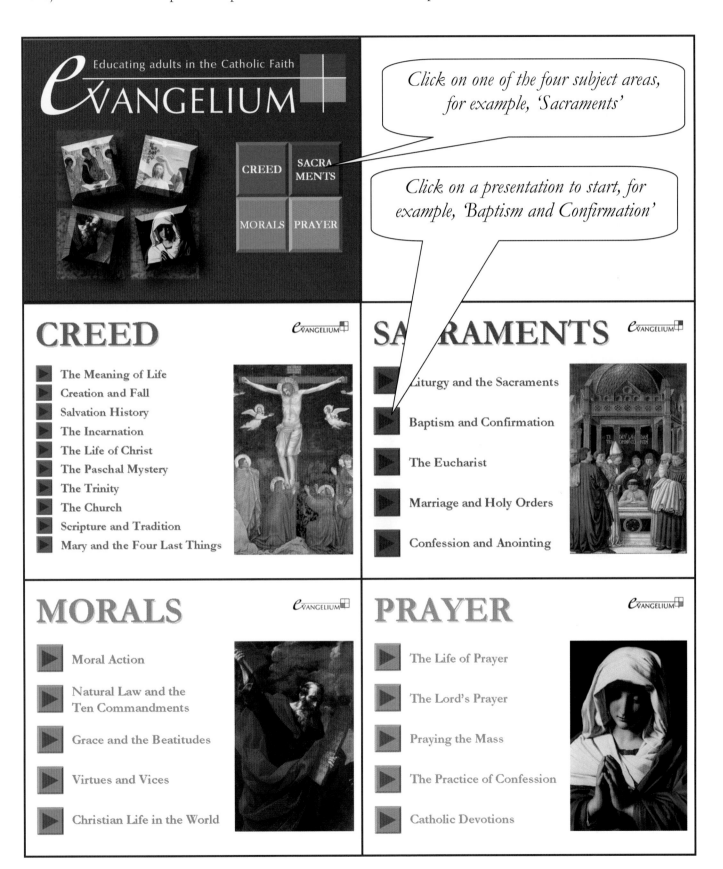

How do I control the sequence of PowerPoint© slides

The EVANGELIUM presentations can be run like any PowerPoint Viewer© presentation, using the 'Page Down' or "Page Up', or 'Right Arrow' and 'Left Arrow' keys to go from one slide to the next.

In addition, there are navigation buttons on the EVANGELIUM slides to provide additional control over the presentation sequence.

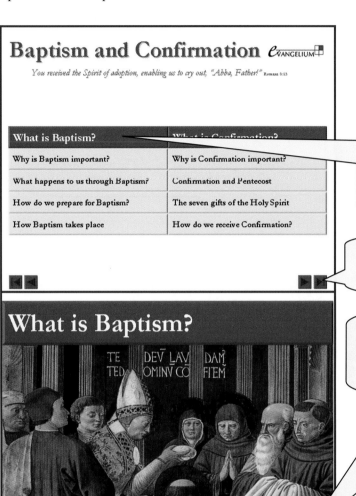

This screen shows the sections of the presentation. Either choose a particular place to start within the presentation…

…or click here to go directly to the first slide

Within the presentation click here to go to the next slide, or press the 'page down' or 'right arrow' key.

Click here to go directly to the next section topic of the presentation

Press 'ESC' on your keyboard at any time to exit the presentation and return to the EVANGELIUM main menus. Press 'ESC' again to close the EVANGELIUM session.

Click here to return to the start of the section

Click here to return to the previous slide

How do I close an EVANGELIUM presentation?

At the conclusion of the presentation and activities click on the ESC key on the keyboard to exit from the session to the EVANGELIUM main menus.

Click on the ESC key a second time to close EVANGELIUM.

Opening Prayer

As the final goal of Christian teaching is to know God, it is good to ask for God's help at the beginning of each session. The following short prayer is from St Thomas Aquinas, who always prayed before study.

Bestow upon me, O God,
an understanding that knows you, wisdom
in finding you, a way of life that is
pleasing to you, perseverance that faithfully
waits for you, and confidence that I shall
embrace you at the last. Amen.

The Meaning of Life

CREED

*E*VANGELIUM

PRESENTER'S GUIDE

Preparation

You may wish to read questions 1-5 of the *Compendium*. You can find additional information in the *Catechism* ccc. 27-43 covering: (i) the desire for God (ccc. 27-30); (ii) ways of coming to know God (ccc. 31-35); (iii) the knowledge of God according to the Church (ccc. 36-38); (iv) how we can speak about God (ccc. 39-43).

Since the philosophical nature of the material in this class is relatively challenging, it would be good to study carefully the arguments in the presentation (p. 1-2 of the *Participant's Book*).

Introduction

> **EXAMPLE** *Welcome to our session on 'The Meaning of Life'. By the end of the session you should know why we speak of a first 'be-cause', what we can know about God by our reason, what is special about human beings and what is the ultimate aim of human existence. Each part will last 25 minutes with 10 further minutes for some summary activities.*

Presentation Part I (25 minutes)

Why?

What is the 'first be-cause'?

What is 'God'?

What does creation teach us about God?

***The School of Athens* by Raphael Sanzio** (1483-1520)

The picture shows the philosophers, literally 'lovers of wisdom', who have searched for true knowledge through reason. At the centre of the scene is found Plato (left) and Aristotle (right) who in ancient times discovered profound truths about God, the soul and the world. Plato, who focussed on the more spiritual world of ideas characteristically points upwards, while Aristotle who discovered the truth of things from what we know in the world, points downward to the ground.

Choice of Summary Activities I (10 minutes)

> **EXAMPLE** *You should now be able to show why we speak of knowing God's existence and what the world can tell us about God. The following activities should help to reinforce this understanding.*

Summary	Questions to reinforce key points
Discussion questions	Practical activities

The presentation offers the choice of the four optional activities shown on the left. You may select any of these or proceed to part II of the presentation.

Regarding the '*Questions to reinforce key points*', the hidden answers to the first question, '*What are two of the ways we can know the existence of God?*' are:

(1) Through the need for a first 'be-cause'
(2) Through the order and beauty of the universe

Conclusion

> **EXAMPLE** *I hope that you feel confident to refer to page 1 of the Participant's Book for the answer to our question 'why?' and the other subjects we have covered. We now go on to examine the uniqueness of human beings and the reasons for our existence.*

Presentation Part II (25 minutes)

What are Human Beings?

What do we want?

Where is happiness found?

What does God offer us?

The Creation of Adam by Michelangelo (1475-1564)

The picture emphasises the nobility of the human creature and the possibility of the gift of a personal relationship with God (highlighted by the fact that God looks into Adam's eyes). The garden of Eden, the terrestrial paradise, is depicted by the green ground. Adam is portrayed as perfect in bodily form. His physical beauty mirrors the beauty of his soul created from the beginning in God's image. God is surrounded by angels; this indicates the heavenly realm. The fingers of God and man meet between heaven and earth showing that man's nature is both physical and spiritual.

Choice of Summary Activities II (10 minutes)

EXAMPLE *At the end of this second part you should be able to explain that human beings search for happiness but that full and lasting happiness can only be found through the gift of God. This introduces us to the need for salvation and God's intervention in our lives which is at the heart of Christianity. The following activities should help to reinforce this understanding.*

Summary	Questions to reinforce key points
Discussion questions	Practical activities

The presentation offers the choice of the four optional activities shown on the left. You may select any of these or proceed to the conclusion.

Regarding the '*Questions to reinforce key points*', the hidden answers to the first questions, '*How do human beings differ from all other living beings on earth?*' are:

(1) We know *what* and *why* things are
(2) We make moral choices
(3) We have language

Conclusion

EXAMPLE *Following this session you should know that God's existence and some of his attributes can be known by reason, the unique meaning of human life and that our pursuit of happiness finds its sole solution in God. I also hope you feel confident to refer to pages 1 and 2 of the Participant's Book for a summary of the subjects this presentation has covered. We shall close with psalm 138 in which we praise God for creating us.*

O Lord, you search me and you know me, you know my resting and my rising, you discern my purpose from afar. You mark when I walk or lie down, all my ways lie open before you…For it was you who created my being, knit me together in my mother's womb. I thank you for the wonder of my being, for the wonders of all your creation. Already you knew my soul, my body held no secret from you when I was being fashioned in secret and molded in the depths of the earth … O search me, God, and know my heart. O test me and know my thoughts. See that I follow not the wrong path and lead me in the path of life eternal.

Optional follow-up activities

You may wish to invite the participants to complete one or more of the following activities themselves:

- Read some of the sections of the *Catechism* on knowing God, especially ccc. 31-35 on ways of coming to know God.

- Write down the reasons why they believe in God and why they think human beings are unique.

- Find, read and pray through Romans 1:16-25 and Wisdom 13:1-19, which are about the knowledge of God from creation and false hopes of happiness from other things.

Creation and Fall

CREED

EVANGELIUM

PRESENTER'S GUIDE

Preparation

You may wish to read questions 51-78 of the *Compendium*. You can find additional information in the *Catechism* ccc. 279-421 covering: (i) the Creator (ccc. 279-324); (ii) heaven and earth (ccc. 325-354); man (ccc. 355-384); the fall (ccc. 385-421).

Since the subject of creation may involve a discussion about the book of Genesis and about evolution it would help to anticipate questions that may arise by some prior reading and study.

Introduction

EXAMPLE *Welcome to our session on 'Creation and Fall'. By the end you should know what we mean by 'creation', what science, philosophy and revelation have to say about it, what is unique about the creation of human beings and what happened to them in the event of the 'fall'. Each part will last 25 minutes with 10 further minutes for some summary activities.*

Presentation Part I (25 minutes)

What is Creation?
What do philosophy and science say?
What is special about human beings?
What was the first state of human beings?

The Expulsion from Paradise by Giovanni di Paolo (1403-1483)

The picture shows God creating the world and the expulsion of Adam and Eve out of the Garden of Eden after the fall. God is surrounded by twelve angels and is clearly distinguished from the cosmos that he is creating. He holds back his cloak to emphasise that he is not part of the created order. The action of pointing with the right hand indicates that it is God who creates the world directly and out of nothing; it also conveys a sense of purpose operating in creation. The expulsion of Adam and Eve from paradise shows one of the consequences of Original Sin.

Choice of Summary Activities I (10 minutes)

EXAMPLE *You should now be able to explain what is meant by 'creation', what philosophy and science say about creation and the characteristics of the first state of human beings. The following activities should help to reinforce this understanding.*

Summary	Questions to reinforce key points
Discussion questions	**Practical activities**

The presentation offers the choice of the four optional activities shown on the left. You may select any of these or proceed to part II of the presentation.

Regarding the '*Questions to reinforce key points*', the hidden answers to the first question, '*What was the first state of human beings?*' are:

(1) Freedom from disordered desires
(2) Bodily immortality
(3) Freedom from suffering
(4) Special gifts of knowledge

Conclusion

EXAMPLE *I hope that you feel confident to refer to page 3 of the Participant's Book for the answer to our question 'what is creation?' and the other subjects we have covered. We now go on to examine the event of the fall and its effects.*

Presentation Part II (25 minutes)

What is the Fall?

What was the event of the fall?

What were the effects of the fall?

Was there hope after the fall?

The Garden of Eden by Jacob de Backer (c. 1560-1590) – *This picture highlights the creation of the first man and women in perfect harmony with God and nature. Scripture says that God walked with them in the garden, showing that they enjoyed the gift of sanctifying grace.*

Madonna with Serpent by Caravaggio (1571-1610) – *This shows Jesus and Mary fulfilling the prophecy of Gen 3:16 by crushing the head of the serpent, which represents the devil. It emphasises that Jesus is the new Adam and Mary, Mother of the Church, is the second Eve. On the right, St Anne, mother of Mary, shows that this promise has come through the generations.*

Choice of Summary Activities II (10 minutes)

EXAMPLE *At the end of this second part you should be able to explain the meaning of the fall, what its effects were and how God still promised a future redemption. The following activities should help to reinforce this understanding.*

Summary	Questions to reinforce key points
Discussion questions	Practical activities

The presentation offers the choice of the four optional activities shown on the left. You may select any of these or proceed to the conclusion.

Regarding the '*Questions to reinforce key points*', the hidden answers to the first questions, '*What do we inherit from Adam?*' are:

(1) Original sin
(2) Concupiscence and disorder
(3) A state without grace

Conclusion

EXAMPLE *Following this session you should know about the meaning of creation, the first state of human beings and the event and effects of the fall. I also hope you feel confident to refer to pages 3 and 4 of the Participant's Book for a summary of the subjects this presentation has covered. We shall close with part of psalm 103.*

Bless the LORD, O my soul, and forget not all his benefits, who forgives all your iniquity, who heals all your diseases, who redeems your life from the pit, who crowns you with steadfast love and mercy, who satisfies you with good as long as you live … He will not always chide, nor will he keep his anger for ever. He does not deal with us according to our sins, nor requite us according to our iniquities. For as the heavens are high above the earth, so great is his steadfast love toward those who fear him; as far as the east is from the west, so far does he remove our transgressions from us. As a father pities his children, so the LORD pities those who fear him … who keep his covenant and remember to do his commandments.

Optional follow-up activities

You may wish to invite the participants to complete one or more of the following activities themselves:

- Read some of the sections of the *Catechism*, especially ccc. 282-289 on creation.
- Write down some of the problems they recognise in the present human condition that arise from the fall.
- Visit a place which clearly shows the beauty of creation. Thank God by praying, for example, Psalm 104.
- Find, read and pray through chapters 1-3 of the Book of Genesis.

Salvation History

PRESENTER'S GUIDE

Preparation

You may wish to read questions 6-8 and 102 of the *Compendium*. You can find additional information in the *Catechism* ccc. 50-64 covering: (i) revelation (ccc. 50-53); (ii) the stages of revelation (ccc. 54-64).

Since this class covers large periods of history and parts of the Old Testament it would be worthwhile to be familiar with the texts referred to in the section on 'Salvation History' in the *Participant's Book*, p. 5-6.

Introduction

> EXAMPLE *Welcome to our session on 'Salvation History'. By the end you should know what is meant by 'salvation history' and its principal stages. Each part will last 25 minutes with 10 further minutes for some summary activities.*

Presentation Part I (25 minutes)

What is Salvation History? (I)

What are the stages of salvation history?

The deeper reason for God's promises

God's covenant with Noah

God's covenant with Abraham

***The Sacrifice of Isaac* by Caravaggio** (1571-1610)

The picture shows the dramatic scene of Abraham attempting to sacrifice his son Isaac in obedience to God's command but being restrained by the angel. Abraham is an image of faith in adversity; he is also an image of God the Father who does not withhold even his own Son for our salvation. In one sense, Isaac represents the innocent Christ. In another sense, the ram that God provides to substitute for Isaac (shown in the corner of the picture) also represents Christ. Like the ram, Christ is the sacrificial victim provided not by man but by God himself.

Choice of Summary Activities I (10 minutes)

> EXAMPLE *You should now be able to speak about the stages in salvation history and the first covenants with Noah and Abraham. The following activities should help to reinforce this understanding.*

Summary	Questions to reinforce key points
Discussion questions	Practical activities

The presentation offers the choice of the four optional activities shown on the left. You may select any of these or proceed to part II of the presentation.

Regarding the '*Questions to reinforce key points*', the hidden answers to the first question, '*What are the main promises that God makes in salvation history?*' are:

(1) The preservation of the world **(2)** The establishment of a chosen people **(3)** The permanent gift of a law and a land **(4)** The founding of an everlasting kingdom **(5)** The coming of a final salvation **(6)** The coming of the *Messiah*

Conclusion

> EXAMPLE *I hope that you feel confident to refer to pages 5 of the Participant's Book for the answer to our question, 'What is salvation history?' We now go on to examine the role of Moses, David, the prophets and John the Baptist in salvation history.*

Presentation Part II (25 minutes)

What is Salvation History? (II)

What was God's covenant through Moses?

What was God's covenant with David?

What did the prophets promise?

Who did John the Baptist herald?

Crossing the Red Sea by Cosimo Rosselli (1439-1507)

This picture shows Israel crossing the Red Sea (Exodus 14), one of the pivotal moments in salvation history. Historically, this event marked Israel's final escape from the pursuit of Pharaoh and slavery in Egypt. Spiritually, it signifies liberation from sin and the birth of the people of Israel as God's chosen people. The crossing of the Red Sea also prefigures the liberation brought by Jesus Christ and symbolises, in particular, the sacrament of Baptism (Catechism ccc. 1221). Moses is depicted on the left bank with his rod which divided and closed the sea. Miriam kneels to his left, with a drum, giving praise to the Lord.

Choice of Summary Activities II (10 minutes)

> **EXAMPLE** *At the end of this second part you should be able to explain the covenants with Moses and David, the importance of the prophets and of John the Baptist. The following activities should help to reinforce this understanding.*

Summary	Questions to reinforce key points
Discussion questions	Practical activities

The presentation offers the choice of the four optional activities shown on the left. You may select any of these or proceed to the conclusion.

Regarding the '*Questions to reinforce key points*', the hidden answers to the first question, '*Who are the main characters associated with the stages of salvation history?*' are:

(1) Noah   (4) David

(2) Abraham   (5) The prophets

(3) Moses   (6) John the Baptist

Conclusion

> **EXAMPLE** *Following this session you should know how God has acted in various ways and through various stages in saving the human race. I also hope you feel confident to refer to pages 5 and 6 of the Participant's Book for a summary of the subjects this presentation has covered. We shall finish by praying psalm 111, which calls to mind the covenant of God with his people.*

I will give thanks to the LORD with my whole heart, in the company of the upright, in the congregation. Great are the works of the LORD, studied by all who have pleasure in them. Full of honor and majesty is his work, and his righteousness endures for ever. He has caused his wonderful works to be remembered; the LORD is gracious and merciful. He provides food for those who fear him; he is ever mindful of his covenant. He has shown his people the power of his works, in giving them the heritage of the nations. The works of his hands are faithful and just; all his precepts are trustworthy, they are established for ever and ever, to be performed with faithfulness and uprightness. He sent redemption to his people; he has commanded his covenant for ever. Holy and terrible is his name! The fear of the LORD is the beginning of wisdom; a good understanding have all those who practice it. His praise endures for ever!

Optional follow-up activities

You may wish to invite the participants to complete one or more of the following activities themselves:

- Read some of the sections of the *Catechism* on salvation history, especially ccc. 50-64, and one or more of the Biblical texts in the relevant section in the *Participant's Book*, p. 5-6.

- Find, read and meditate upon the Fourth Eucharistic Prayer from the Mass. This recalls the events of salvation history culminating in Jesus Christ.

- Find, read and pray through psalms 106 and 136, both of which are prayers that draw on some of the main events of salvation history.

The Incarnation

PRESENTER'S GUIDE

Preparation

You may wish to read questions 79-104 of the *Compendium*. You can find additional information in the *Catechism* ccc. 422-486, especially (i) the titles of Jesus Christ (ccc. 430-455); (ii) true and false beliefs about the Incarnation (ccc. 461-483).

Introduction

EXAMPLE *Welcome to our session on 'The Incarnation'. By the end you should know what is meant by the word 'Incarnation', the way Christ came to be born and his titles. You should also be able to understand the Church's doctrinal definitions about the Incarnation and the reasons why certain positions are excluded.*

Each part will last 25 minutes with 10 further minutes for some summary activities.

Presentation Part I (25 minutes)

What is the Incarnation?

How did Jesus Christ come to be born?

What are the titles of Jesus Christ?

***The Annunciation* by Fra Angelico** (c. 1400-1455) – *This picture of the Annunciation shows the moment of the Incarnation. Mary responds in humble assent to the message of the Angel Gabriel whose words appear as a scroll. The presence of God the Father is symbolised by the sculpture above the pillar; the presence of God the Son by the words and the presence of God the Holy Spirit by the dove. The veil being drawn back implies revelation; the fruitfulness of the garden represents the effects of Christ's coming. This is in contrast to the barren landscape in the distant background, which represents the separation of Adam and Eve from God and their expulsion from paradise.*

Choice of Summary Activities I (10 minutes)

EXAMPLE *You should now be able to explain what is meant by the Incarnation and also how Jesus came to be born. You should also understand the titles of Jesus. The following activities should help to reinforce this understanding.*

Summary	Questions to reinforce key points
Discussion questions	Practical activities

The presentation offers the choice of the four optional activities shown on the left. You may select any of these or proceed to part II of the presentation.

Regarding the '*Questions to reinforce key points*', the hidden answers to the first question, '*What are the main titles of Jesus?*' are:

(1) Jesus
(2) Christ
(3) Lord
(4) Son of God
(5) Son of Man
(6) Son of David

Conclusion

EXAMPLE *I hope that you feel confident to refer to page 7 of the Participant's Book for the answer to our question, what is the Incarnation. We now go on to examine the Church's doctrinal definitions of the Incarnation.*

Presentation Part II (25 minutes)

True God and True Man	*The Nativity* **by Petrus Christus** (c. 1410-1476) – *This painting includes symbols of many aspects of the Incarnation. Jesus lies on the untainted mantle of Mary rather than on the barren soil of the fallen world, symbolising the freedom of Mary from sin. The figures of Adam and Eve emphasise the human nature of Jesus Christ; his adoration by Joseph and the angels symbolises his divinity. The scenes from salvation history around the image present the Incarnation as the culmination of God's plan for our salvation. The triangle on the upper structure of the barn symbolises the Trinity. The candle above the sacred head of the child indicates the coming of Jesus Christ as the 'light of the world'.*
The Incarnation in the Creed	
The Incarnation and the *Hail Mary*	

Choice of Summary Activities II (10 minutes)

> EXAMPLE *At the end of this second part you should be able to explain why we call Jesus Christ 'true God and true man', why certain beliefs about Jesus Christ are in error and also how the great prayer 'The Hail Mary' is linked to the Incarnation. The following activities should help to reinforce this understanding.*

Summary	**Questions to reinforce key points**
Discussion questions	**Practical activities**

The presentation offers the choice of the four optional activities shown on the left. You may select any of these or proceed to the conclusion.

Regarding the '*Questions to reinforce key points*', the hidden answers to the first question, '*What does the Creed say about Jesus Christ and the Incarnation?*' are:

(1) The only Son of God … begotten, not made, one in Being with the Father.
(2) Through him all things were made.
(3) For us men and for our salvation he came down from heaven.
(4) He become incarnate of the Virgin Mary, and was made man.

Conclusion

> EXAMPLE *Following this session you should know what the Incarnation means and how the teaching that Jesus Christ is true God and true man should be understood. I also hope you feel confident to refer to pages 7 and 8 of the Participant's Book for a summary of the subjects this presentation has covered.*
>
> *We shall close with a translation of the words of the Ave Verum Corpus, an ancient hymn possibly written by Pope Innocent VI. Although it is just five lines long, it covers the Incarnation, the Passion, the Eucharist and the Last Judgment. Many, including some of the greatest of all composers, have set the Ave Verum Corpus to music.*

Hail true body born of the Virgin Mary,	*Ave verum corpus natum de Maria Virgine*
That truly suffered and was sacrificed on the Cross for men,	*vere passum immolatum in cruce pro homine*
From whose pierced side flowed water and blood;	*cuius latum perforatum fluxit aqua et sanguine*
Be for us a foretaste of death and judgment.	*esto nobis praegustatum mortis in examine*
O sweet Jesus! O gentle Jesus! O Jesus, son of Mary.	*O Iesu dulcis! O Iesu pie! O Iesu fili Mariae.*

Optional follow-up activities

You may wish to invite the participants to complete one or more of the following activities themselves:

* Read some sections of the *Catechism* on the Incarnation, especially ccc. 430-455 on the titles of Jesus.
* Ask family and friends the question about who they think that Jesus Christ is. Point out that this is what Jesus asked his own disciples (Matthew 16:15) and invite them to read Peter's response.
* Find, read and pray through the infancy narratives in Matthew 1:18-2:23 and Luke 1-2.

The Life of Christ

Preparation

You may wish to read questions 105-111 of the *Compendium*. You can find additional information in the *Catechism* ccc. 512-570, especially: (i) the mysteries of Jesus' infancy and hidden life (ccc. 522-534); (ii) the mysteries of Jesus' public life (ccc. 535-570).

It is possible that questions regarding the reliability of Gospel evidence may arise. If your group is one that likes discussions of this kind, you may wish to consult a work of apologetics as well.

Introduction

EXAMPLE *Welcome to our session on 'The Life of Christ'. By the end you should know the stages of Christ's life, what he has done and the various ways we know him. Each part will last 25 minutes with 10 further minutes for some summary activities.*

Presentation Part I (25 minutes)

What is the Life of Christ?

The principal events of the life of Christ

Jesus' ministry: identity and mission

Jesus' ministry: doctrine and Church

***Triumphal Entry* by Giotto di Bondone** (1267-1337)
This picture shows the dramatic entry of Jesus into Jerusalem before his sacred Passion and death. The crowd recognise him and hail him as the Messiah with the words, "Hosanna to the Son of David." (Mt 21:15). They lay their garments down before his path. Yet in a few days they will call for his crucifixion and death (Mt 27:23). Literally, these events fulfil the many prophecies of Scripture that Jesus would be rejected. Spiritually, this triumphal entry prefigures the coming of Christ into the Heavenly Jerusalem, where he shall reign with his saints for ever.

Choice of Summary Activities I (10 minutes)

EXAMPLE *You should now know the principal stages of the life of Jesus Christ and the main aspects of his public mission. The following activities should help to reinforce this understanding.*

Summary	Questions to reinforce key points
Discussion questions	Practical activities

The presentation offers the choice of the four optional activities shown on the left. You may select any of these or proceed to part II of the presentation.

Regarding the '*Questions to reinforce key points*', the hidden answers to the first question, '*What are the principal stages of the life of Christ?*' are:

(1) Conception and birth
(2) Hidden life
(3) Public ministry
(4) Death, Resurrection and Ascension

Conclusion

EXAMPLE *I hope that you feel confident to refer to page 9 of the Participant's Book for the answer to our question 'What is the life of Christ?' and the other subjects we have covered. We now go on to examine the ways in which we can know Jesus Christ.*

Presentation Part II (25 minutes)

Knowing Jesus Christ
Knowing Jesus Christ through reason
Knowing Jesus Christ through faith
Knowing Jesus Christ personally

The Calling of Saint Matthew **by Caravaggio** (1571-1610)

Matthew sits at his counting desk as a tax collector, but a light illuminates his face as Christ enters. He points to himself in disbelief and looks like someone caught committing a crime (his right hand is still counting the money with two oblivious assistants). The hand of Christ pointing at him is the same shape as the famous hand of God in Michelangelo's creation of Adam. This shows us that Jesus Christ is indeed God upon earth. The picture also emphasises the very individual nature of conversion and how each one of us is called to know and follow Christ personally.

Choice of Summary Activities II (10 minutes)

> EXAMPLE *At the end of this second part you should be able to explain the distinct ways in which we can know Jesus Christ. The following activities should help to reinforce this understanding.*

Summary	Questions to reinforce key points
Discussion questions	Practical activities

The presentation offers the choice of the four optional activities shown on the left. You may select any of these or proceed to the conclusion.

Regarding the '*Questions to reinforce key points*', the hidden answers to the first questions, '*What are the three ways in which we can know Jesus Christ?*' are:

(1) Through reason
(2) Through faith
(3) Personally

Conclusion

> EXAMPLE *Following this session you should know the main events and significance of Jesus' life and also the ways in which we can know him. I also hope you feel confident to refer to pages 9 and 10 of the Participant's Book for a summary of the subjects this presentation has covered.*
>
> *We shall close with the words of the last two verses of a famous hymn, St Patrick's Breastplate.*

> *Christ be with me, Christ within me, Christ behind me, Christ before me, Christ beside me, Christ to win me, Christ to comfort and restore me. Christ beneath me, Christ above me, Christ in quiet, Christ in danger, Christ in hearts of all that love me, Christ in mouth of friend and stranger.*
>
> *I bind unto myself the name, the strong name of the Trinity, by invocation of the same, the Three in One and One in Three. By whom all nature hath creation, Eternal Father, Spirit, Word: praise to the Lord of my salvation, salvation is of Christ the Lord.*

Optional follow-up activities

You may wish to invite the participants to complete one or more of the following activities themselves:

- Read some of the sections of the *Catechism* on Jesus' life, especially ccc. 512-570.
- Examine how they themselves know Jesus Christ according to each of the three ways.
- Choose one Gospel and begin a programme of reading it all the way through.

The Paschal Mystery

PRESENTER'S GUIDE

Preparation

You may wish to read questions 112-132 of the *Compendium*. You can find additional information in the *Catechism* ccc. 571-667, especially: (i) Christ's redemptive death in God's plan of salvation (ccc. 599-605); (ii) Christ's offering of himself to the Father for our sins (ccc. 606-623); (iii) Christ's descent into hell (ccc. 632-637); (iv) his rising from the dead (ccc. 638-658); (v) his Ascension into heaven (ccc. 659-667).

Since some of the concepts surrounding the Paschal mystery are complex and multi-sided it would be worth reading the *Participant's Book* p. 11-12 with special care before embarking upon this class.

Introduction

EXAMPLE *Welcome to our session on 'The Paschal Mystery'. By the end you should know the meaning of the Paschal mystery, what it achieves for the world and its implications for every human being. You should also learn about the meaning of Jesus' Ascension. Each part will last 25 minutes with 10 further minutes for some summary activities.*

Presentation Part I (25 minutes)

The Passion of Jesus

What is the Passion of Jesus Christ?

What were the events of the Passion?

What is the atonement?

The atonement and ourselves

The Crucifixion by Giotto di Bondone (1267-1337) – *The picture shows the historical and theological dimensions of Christ's Passion. The angels catching the precious blood of Christ in cups or chalices emphasise that this is a sacrificial offering and also make the link with the Mass explicit. The presence of both contemporary and later historical figures praying at the foot of the cross (most noticeably St Francis and his friars on the right) shows that this sacrifice is for the salvation of the human race across all times and places. The angels express the sorrow and awe that the beholder should feel before this mystery. The centurion (centre-right), whose hands are joined, is being brought to faith by the event.*

Choice of Summary Activities I (10 minutes)

EXAMPLE *You should now be able to explain the meaning of the Passion and how it brings about atonement for sin and re-union between God and humanity. The following activities should help to reinforce this understanding.*

Summary	Questions to reinforce key points
Discussion questions	Practical activities

The presentation offers the choice of the four optional activities shown on the left. You may select any of these or proceed to part II of the presentation.

Regarding the *'Questions to reinforce key points'*, the hidden answers to the first question, *'What does the atonement do for us?'* are:

(1) Fulfils Scripture and salvation history

(2) Reconciles us to God

(3) Defeats the claims of the devil over us

(4) Repays our debt of guilt

(5) Gains mercy for us and repeals our punishment

Conclusion

EXAMPLE *I hope that you feel confident to refer to page 11 of the Participant's Book for the definition of the Paschal mystery, and the other subjects we have covered. We now go on to examine the completion of the Paschal mystery in the historical event of the Resurrection and the Ascension.*

Presentation Part II (25 minutes)

The Resurrection of Jesus

The descent to the dead

What is the Resurrection?

The importance of the Resurrection for us

What is the Ascension?

The Resurrection by Piero della Francesca (c. 1416-1492)

This picture shows the triumphant nature of Jesus' Resurrection. He stands with a banner of victory with his enemies beneath his feet. He is a perfect figure of humanity for the artist, solid, confident yet restrained. The contrast of the dead wood in the background on the left with the evergreens on the right symbolises his triumph over death and his rising to eternal life. The wounds still present in the hands, feet and side of Christ emphasise the physical reality of his risen body and the enduring value of his offering for the world.

Choice of Summary Activities II (10 minutes)

EXAMPLE *At the end of this second part you should be able to explain the meaning of the descent of Jesus Christ to the dead, his Resurrection and his Ascension. You should also be able to explain the theological significance of the Resurrection and why it is an historical and physical event. The following activities should help to reinforce this understanding.*

Summary	Questions to reinforce key points
Discussion questions	Practical activities

The presentation offers the choice of the four optional activities shown on the left. You may select any of these or proceed to the conclusion.

Regarding the '*Questions to reinforce key points*', the hidden answers to the first questions, '*What does Jesus confirm by his Resurrection?*' are:

(1) Human life does not cease with death

(2) Promise of a glorified risen humanity

(3) Validation of all he taught and did

Conclusion

EXAMPLE *Following this session you should know the meaning and importance of the Paschal mystery through the Passion, death and Resurrection of Jesus Christ. I also hope you feel confident to refer to pages 11 and 12 of the Participant's Book for a summary of the subjects this presentation has covered. We shall close with one of the prayers from the Chaplet of Divine Mercy.*

You expired Jesus but the source of life gushed forth for the whole world and the ocean of mercy opened up for the whole world. O, fount of life, unfathomable Divine Mercy, envelope the whole world and empty yourself out upon us.

Optional follow-up activities

You may wish to invite the participants to complete one or more of the following activities themselves:

* Read some of the sections of the *Catechism* on the Paschal mystery, such as ccc. 571-667.

* Visit a local Catholic church and note down any symbols of the Paschal mystery that they see and any special aspects of these symbols that they notice.

* Find and write down a list of the Stations of the Cross.

* Pray the Sorrowful and Glorious Mysteries of the Rosary (you may have to introduce this to them if they are not already familiar with it).

* Find, read and pray through one of the Passion narratives in the Gospels.

The Trinity

Preparation

You may wish to read questions 33-50 and 136-146 of the *Compendium*. You can find additional information in the *Catechism* ccc. 199-267 and ccc. 683-747, especially: (i) belief in God (ccc. 199-231); (ii) the revelation of God as Trinity (ccc. 238-248); (iii) the Holy Trinity in the teaching of the faith (ccc. 249-256); (iv) the divine works and Trinitarian missions (ccc. 257-260); (v) belief in the Holy Spirit (ccc. 683-686).

Since the Trinity is a difficult subject it would be worth reading the *Participant's Book* p. 13-14 with special care before embarking upon this class.

Introduction

EXAMPLE *Welcome to our session on 'The Trinity'. By the end you should know the essential teaching about the Trinity, the Trinitarian structure of the Creed, our Christian relationship to the Trinity and common mistakes about the Trinity.*

Each part will last 25 minutes with 10 further minutes for some summary activities.

Presentation Part I (25 minutes)

The Revelation of the Trinity

The revelation of the one God

The revelation of the three persons

The Trinity in Creed and worship

The Holy Trinity with Mary Magdalene, St. John the Baptist and Tobias and the Angel by **Alessandro Botticelli** (1445-1510) – *This shows the unity of the three divine persons in the work of our salvation. The crucified human nature of the incarnate Son, Jesus Christ, is in the foreground. The Father supports the cross and offers his Son for our salvation. Their union is in the love of the Holy Spirit, represented by the dove. The order of these symbols shows how our knowledge of the Trinity has come to us exclusively through Jesus Christ. Without his Incarnation, the immortal and invisible Trinity would be unknown and unknowable to us. St John the Baptist on the right bears witness to Christ and calls for our worship of the mystery.*

Choice of Summary Activities I (10 minutes)

EXAMPLE *You should now know that the one God has revealed himself as three persons and how the Creed has a Trinitarian structure. The following activities should help to reinforce this understanding.*

Summary	Questions to reinforce key points
Discussion questions	Practical activities

The presentation offers the choice of the four optional activities shown on the left. You may select any of these or proceed to part II of the presentation.

Regarding the '*Questions to reinforce key points*', the hidden answers to the first question, '*What are the two essential elements of the doctrine of the Trinity?*' are:

(1) One God
(2) Three persons

Conclusion

EXAMPLE *I hope that you feel confident to refer to page 13 of the Participant's Book for an explanation of how the Trinity is revealed to us. We now go on to examine the meaning of the Trinitarian doctrine and how the Trinity relates to us.*

Presentation Part II (25 minutes)

What is the Trinity?

One substance, three persons

Mistaken beliefs about the Trinity

The Trinity and our friendship with God

The Trinity by **Andrei Rublev** (c. 1360-1430) – *The picture attempts to show what is impossible to depict, the eternal and immanent Trinity: Father, Son and Holy Spirit. The persons are shown in a perfect communion. The equality of their forms shows that they are equally the one God, but the positions of their eyes distinguish their relationships. The Father is on the left, the Son is in the middle with his two hands on the table pointing to the cup of sacrifice, and the Holy Spirit is on the right. Each holds a staff indicating his divine power. The open table and chalice pointing towards the foreground is an invitation to the viewer to enter into the divine life of the Trinity, especially through the Eucharist.*

Choice of Summary Activities II (10 minutes)

EXAMPLE *At the end of this second part you should be able to explain why we speak of 'one substance, three persons', to list the mistaken beliefs about the Trinity and to state how the Trinity relates to us in the Christian life.*

The following activities should help to reinforce this understanding.

Summary	Questions to reinforce key points
Discussion questions	Practical activities

The presentation offers the choice of the four optional activities shown on the left. You may select any of these or proceed to the conclusion.

Regarding the '*Questions to reinforce key points*', the hidden answers to the first questions, '*How does the Trinity relate to us?*' are:

(1) All Christian belief is Trinitarian

(2) All sacraments are Trinitarian

(3) All Christian life is directed towards union with the Trinity

(4) All Christian prayer is Trinitarian

Conclusion

EXAMPLE *Following this session you should know how the Trinity has been revealed to us and how we speak about the Trinity. I also hope you feel confident to refer to pages 13 and 14 of the Participant's Book for a summary of the subjects this presentation has covered. We shall close with part of an ancient Trinitarian prayer of praise, the Te Deum.*

We praise you, O God: we acclaim you as the Lord. Everlasting Father, all the world bows down before you. All the angels sing your praise, the hosts of heaven and all the angelic powers, all the cherubim and seraphim call out to you in unending song: Holy, Holy, Holy, is the Lord God of angel hosts. The heavens and the earth are filled with your majesty and glory. The glorious band of apostles, the noble company of prophets, the white-robed army who shed their blood for Christ, all sing your praise. And to the ends of the earth your holy Church proclaims her faith in you: Father, whose majesty is boundless, your true and only Son who is to be adored. The Holy Spirit sent to be our Advocate.

Optional follow-up activities

You may wish to invite the participants to complete one or more of the following activities themselves:

- Read some of the sections of the *Catechism* on the Trinity, especially ccc. 199-267 on the persons of God and ccc. 687-747 on the Holy Spirit.

- Learn a Trinitarian prayer, such as the Sign of the Cross if they do not already know this, the Creed or part or all of the *Te Deum*.

- Find, read and pray through one or more of the following passages of Scripture which refer to the three divine persons: Matthew 28:18-20; Mark 1:9-11; Luke 1:35; John 14:25-31; Galatians 4:4-7.

The Church

Preparation

You may wish to read questions 147-195 of the *Compendium*. You can find additional information in the *Catechism*, ccc. 748-962, especially: (i) the Church's origin, foundation and mission (ccc. 758-769); (ii) the mystery of the Church (ccc. 770-780); (iii) the Church as one, holy, catholic and apostolic (ccc. 811-870); (iv) the hierarchy, laity and consecrated life (ccc. 871-945); (v) the communion of saints (ccc. 946-962).

Since questions may arise regarding other Christian communities, it is worth being aware of their different views and where they stand in relation to the Catholic Church (p. 15-16 of the *Participant's Book*).

Introduction

> **EXAMPLE** *Welcome to our session on 'The Church'. By the end of this session you should know how and why Jesus established a Church and be able to recognize its essential characteristics.*
>
> *Each part will last 25 minutes with 10 further minutes for some summary activities.*

Presentation Part I (25 minutes)

What is the Church?

The Church in the Creed

The foundation of the Church by Christ

Mistakes about the Church

***Christ handing the keys to St Peter* by Pietro Perugino** (1450-1523) – *This picture shows us the founding event of the Church on earth. Jesus gives the keys of the kingdom to St Peter (Mt 16:18-19), in the midst of the other apostles, saying that whatever he binds on earth shall be bound in heaven, and whatever he looses on earth shall be loosed in heaven. The keys are the symbol of the supreme authority of Peter and of his successors, the Popes. The office of binding and loosing which was given to Peter was also assigned to the college of apostles united to its head. This pastoral authority is continued today by the bishops under the primacy of the Pope.*

Choice of Summary Activities I (10 minutes)

> **EXAMPLE** *You should now know what the Church is, its characteristics and how it was founded. The following activities should help to reinforce this understanding.*

Summary	Questions to reinforce key points
Discussion questions	Practical activities

The presentation offers the choice of the four optional activities shown on the left. You may select any of these or proceed to part II of the presentation.

Regarding the '*Questions to reinforce key points*', the hidden answers to the first question, '*What are the four marks of the Church?*' are:

(1) One
(2) Holy
(3) Catholic
(4) Apostolic

Conclusion

> **EXAMPLE** *I hope that you feel confident to refer to page 15 of the Participant's Book for a definition of the Church. We now go on to examine the where the Church of Christ is found.*

Presentation Part II (25 minutes)

Where is the Church?

The Church on earth

The Church in purgatory

The Church in heaven

The San Marco altarpiece by Fra Angelico (c. 1400-1455)

The picture highlights the Church in glory in heaven; all are gathered around Christ and Mary, the Mother of the Church. The saints are interceding for us here on earth. The evergreen trees in the background symbolise the eternity of heaven. The kneeling Ss Cosmas and Damian are shown in the front. In the second row, from the left are Ss Lawrence, John the Evangelist, Mark, Dominic, Francis and Peter Martyr. The distinctiveness of these figures highlights how the saints have their own, proper glory in the Church in heaven.

Choice of Summary Activities II (10 minutes)

EXAMPLE *At the end of this second part you should be able to explain where the Church exists and something about its structure. You should know the meaning of 'the communion of saints' and also the difference between the Catholic Church and other Christian churches and ecclesial communities. The following activities should help to reinforce this understanding.*

Summary	Questions to reinforce key points
Discussion questions	Practical activities

The presentation offers the choice of the four optional activities shown on the left. You may select any of these or proceed to the conclusion.

Regarding the *'Questions to reinforce key points'*, the hidden answers to the first questions, *'Where is the Church?'* are:

(1) On earth

(2) In purgatory

(3) In heaven

Conclusion

EXAMPLE *Following this session you should know what the Church is and where to find her. I also hope you feel confident to refer to pages 15 and 16 of the Participant's Book for a summary of the subjects this presentation has covered.*

We shall close with the words from two verses of a famous hymn celebrating the Church in heaven, 'Jerusalem the Golden'. In Scripture, 'Jerusalem' is often a spiritual symbol of the Church.

Jerusalem the golden, with milk and honey blest, Beneath thy contemplation sink heart and voice oppressed.
I know not, O I know not, what joys await us there, What radiancy of glory, what bliss beyond compare.

O sweet and blessed country, the home of God's elect! O sweet and blessed country, that eager hearts expect!
Jesus, in mercy bring us to that dear land of rest, Who art, with God the Father, and Spirit, ever blessed.

Optional follow-up activities

You may wish to invite the participants to complete one or more of the following activities themselves:

- Read some of the sections of the *Catechism* on the Catholic Church, especially ccc. 748-962.

- Carry out some historical research on the Church. One way of organising this might be to draw a two thousand year timeline and mark the dates of a few of the most important events, the most famous Popes and most famous saints.

- Find, read and pray through one or more of the following passages of Scripture about the Church: Matthew 16:18-19; Colossians 1:13-29; Ephesians 3:1-21.

Scripture and Tradition

Preparation

You may wish to read questions 6-24 of the *Compendium*. You can find additional information in the *Catechism* ccc. 74-141, especially: (i) the Apostolic Tradition (ccc. 75-79); (ii) the relationship of Tradition and Scripture (ccc. 80-83); (iii) the interpretation of the heritage of faith (ccc. 84-100); Sacred Scripture (ccc. 101-141).

Since the idea of Tradition may be easily misunderstood, it is important to try to grasp its principles clearly beforehand (p. 17-18 of the *Participant's Book*).

Introduction

EXAMPLE *Welcome to our session on 'Scripture and Tradition'. By the end you should know the meaning and relationship of Scripture, Tradition and the Magisterium. Each part will last 25 minutes with 10 further minutes for some summary activities.*

Presentation Part I (25 minutes)

Scripture and Tradition (I)

What is Scripture?

What is Tradition?

What is the Magisterium?

Saint Matthew writing his Gospel by **Caravaggio** (1571-1610) – *This picture emphasises the fact that in the writing of Scripture there is both a human author and a divine author, God himself. Here the angel brings to St Matthew's mind the details that he must include in his Gospel, a fulfilment of the promise of Jesus to his disciples that 'the Holy Spirit, whom the Father will send in my name, he will teach you all things, and bring to your remembrance all that I have said to you.' (Jn 14:26). At the same time, St Matthew is not taking dictation. It is also his own work with his own experiences and style. Matthew has one foot on the earth and one off the ground, indicating both the earthly and heavenly influences behind the evangelist.*

Choice of Summary Activities I (10 minutes)

EXAMPLE *You should now be able to show why we speak of Scripture, Tradition and the Magisterium together. The following activities should help to reinforce this understanding.*

Summary	Questions to reinforce key points
Discussion questions	Practical activities

The presentation offers the choice of the four optional activities shown on the left. You may select any of these or proceed to part II of the presentation.

Regarding the '*Questions to reinforce key points*', the hidden answers to the first question, '*By what three interlocking principles do we know God's revelation?*' are:

(1) Scripture
(2) Tradition
(3) Magisterium

Conclusion

EXAMPLE *I hope that you feel confident to refer to page 17 of the Participant's Book for the answer to our questions on the meaning of Scripture, Tradition and the Magisterium. We now go on to examine how we read and interpret Scripture.*

Presentation Part II (25 minutes)

Scripture and Tradition (II)

The structure of the Bible

This page in the Participant's Book has no picture, but instead has a diagram showing the major divisions of the Bible into the Old and New Testaments and the kinds of works found in each of these.

How do I navigate Scripture?

The authentic reading of Scripture

Choice of Summary Activities II (10 minutes)

EXAMPLE *At the end of this second part you should be able to navigate your way around the Bible and understand the principles of Catholic interpretation. The following activities should help to reinforce this understanding.*

Summary	Questions to reinforce key points
Discussion questions	Practical activities

The presentation offers the choice of the four optional activities shown on the left. You may select any of these or proceed to the conclusion.

Regarding the '*Questions to reinforce key points*', the hidden answers to the first questions, '*How do I read the Scripture authentically?*' are:

(1) Read as one

(2) Read within the Tradition

(3) Read in a literal sense

(4) Read in a spiritual sense

Conclusion

EXAMPLE *Following this session you should know how God's revelation is found in Scripture and Tradition. I also hope you feel confident to refer to pages 17 and 18 of the Participant's Book for a summary of the subjects this presentation has covered.*

We shall close with the Apostles' Creed. This is one of the first and most important formulations of the central truths of Tradition, drawn from Scripture and affirmed by the authority of the Magisterium.

I believe in God, the Father Almighty, Creator of heaven and earth.

I believe in Jesus Christ, his only son, our Lord. He was conceived by the power of the Holy Spirit and born of the Virgin Mary. He suffered under Pontius Pilate, was crucified, died and was buried. He descended into hell. On the third day he rose again. He ascended into heaven and is seated at the right hand of the Father. He will come again to judge the living and the dead.

I believe in the Holy Spirit, the holy Catholic Church, the communion of saints, the forgiveness of sins, the resurrection of the body, and life everlasting. Amen.

Optional follow-up activities

You may wish to invite the participants to complete one or more of the following activities themselves:

- Read some of the sections of the *Catechism* on Scripture and Tradition, especially ccc. 74-141 on Scripture, Tradition and the Magisterium and ccc. 888-892 on the teaching office of the Church.

- Learn the names and orders of some of the key books of the Bible, such as: the names of the first five books of the Old Testament; the names and order of the four Gospels; the main categories of the books of the Old and New Testaments (in the chart on p. 18 of the *Participant's Book*).

- Find, read and pray through 2 Thessalonians 2:14-17, 2 Timothy 3:14-17 and Luke 24:13-35.

Mary and the Four Last Things

PRESENTER'S GUIDE

EVANGELIUM

Preparation

You may wish to read questions 94-100, 133-135, 196-199 and 202-216 of the *Compendium*. You can find additional information in the *Catechism* ccc. 963-1060 especially: (i) Mary as the mother of Christ (ccc. 963-975); (ii) Mary as the mother of the Church (ccc. 988-1060); (iii) the resurrection of the body (ccc. 988-1019); (iv) life everlasting (ccc. 1020-1060).

Since some participants may have queries regarding the Catholic teaching on Mary, it would be helpful to read carefully the teaching in the *Catechism* and in the *Participant's Book*, p. 19-20.

Introduction

> **EXAMPLE** *Welcome to our session on 'Mary and the Four Last Things'. By the end you should know the importance of Mary in Christian faith and life and also the meaning of death, judgment, heaven and hell. Each part will last 25 minutes with 10 further minutes for some summary activities.*

Presentation Part I (25 minutes)

Mary, the Mother of Jesus

Why is she called 'Mother of God'?

Why is she called the 'Virgin Mary'?

What is the Immaculate Conception?

What is her Assumption?

The importance of Mary for us

The Coronation of the Virgin by **Enguerrand Quarton** (c. 1410-1461) – *This picture shows Mary crowned by the Blessed Trinity, Father Son and Holy Spirit. She is surrounded by the heavenly court and by angels. She is crowned as Queen of Heaven and shown as the glory of the creation, the sinless and faithful one who gave birth to the second person of the Blessed Trinity as man. The saving death of Christ which opens the way to heaven for all people, including Mary, is at the centre of the picture below the Virgin. The picture also shows the final states of heaven and hell and as well as purgatory. The city on the left of the picture is Rome and the one on the right is Jerusalem, the two holy cities in the present world which are at the heart of the drama of salvation.*

Choice of Summary Activities I (10 minutes)

> **EXAMPLE** *You should now be able to show why Mary has such an important place in Christianity. The following activities should help to reinforce this understanding.*

Summary	Questions to reinforce key points
Discussion questions	Practical activities

The presentation offers the choice of the four optional activities shown on the left. You may select any of these or proceed to part II of the presentation.

Regarding the '*Questions to reinforce key points*', the hidden answers to the first question, '*What are the main events of Mary's life?*' are:

(1) Immaculate Conception
(2) Annunciation
(3) The Virgin Birth
(4) Faithfulness at the cross
(5) Presence at Pentecost
(6) Assumption

Conclusion

> **EXAMPLE** *I hope that you feel confident to refer to page 19 of the Participant's Book to understand Catholic teaching on Mary. We now go on to examine the meaning of the 'Four Last Things'.*

Presentation Part II (25 minutes)

The Four Last Things

What are the four last things?

What is death?

What is judgment?

What is heaven?

What is hell?

Details from *The Seven Deadly Sins* by Hieronymous Bosch (1450-1516)

These details from Bosch show in dramatic fashion the two inevitable and the two alternative realities that we face at the end of our earthly lives. In the depiction of death we see a sick man who is being tended to by his family and by a priest. Above his bed an angel and a demon vie for his soul. The Last Judgment is shown by Christ coming and raising the dead from their tombs. Heaven is depicted as a glorious city filled with angels and saints. Hell is shown as a place of torment, pain, darkness and egoism.

Choice of Summary Activities II (10 minutes)

EXAMPLE *At the end of this second part you should be able to explain the meaning and the importance of the Four Last Things. The following activities should help to reinforce this understanding.*

Summary	Questions to reinforce key points
Discussion questions	Practical activities

The presentation offers the choice of the four optional activities shown on the left. You may select any of these or proceed to the conclusion.

Regarding the '*Questions to reinforce key points*', the hidden answers to the first questions, '*What are the four last things?*' are:

(1) Death

(2) Judgment

(3) Heaven

(4) Hell

Conclusion

EXAMPLE *Following this session you should know the main elements of Catholic teaching about Mary and the Four Last Things. I also hope you feel confident to refer to pages 19 and 20 of the Participant's Book for a summary of the subjects this presentation has covered.*

We shall close with the 'Hail Holy Queen', a prayer for the intercession of Mary to aid our pilgrimage through this earthly life towards our salvation. This prayer also reminds us of the glorious life that is offered to us after this 'vale of tears'.

Hail Holy Queen, mother of mercy. Hail our life, our sweetness, and our hope. To thee do we cry, poor banished children of Eve. To thee do we send up our sighs, mourning and weeping in this vale of tears. Turn, then, most gracious advocate, thine eyes of mercy toward us. And after this, our exile, show unto us the blessed fruit of thy womb, Jesus. O clement, O loving, O sweet Virgin Mary. Pray for us, O holy Mother of God, that we may be made worthy of the promises of Christ. Amen.

Optional follow-up activities

You may wish to invite the participants to complete one or more of the following activities themselves:

* Read some sections of the *Catechism*, especially ccc. 964-970 on Mary's motherhood of the Church and ccc. 988-1060 on the Four Last Things.

* Learn the words of the *Hail Mary*, the *Hail Holy Queen* and the structure of the Rosary if they do not already know these. Invite them to pray the Rosary.

* Visit a local Catholic Church and note any symbols of Mary that they see, such as statues, paintings, inscriptions and stained glass windows. Point out that many statues of Mary show a serpent beneath her feet, symbolising the victory over sin and the devil.

Liturgy and Sacraments

PRESENTER'S GUIDE

Preparation

You may wish to read questions 218-250 of the *Compendium*. You can find additional information in the *Catechism* ccc. 1066-1209 especially: (i) the liturgy in general (ccc. 1066-1112); (ii) the sacraments in general (ccc. 1113-1134); (iii) the celebration of sacramental liturgy (ccc. 1135-1209).

Liturgy and sacraments are familiar experiences for many people. It would therefore be good to find ways of connecting the participants' own experiences with the teaching of this lesson. For example, it might be good to mention some aspects of the liturgy at a local Catholic church to illustrate certain points.

Note that some of the optional practical activities require a Missal, Lectionary or the Divine Office.

Introduction

EXAMPLE *Welcome to our session on 'Liturgy and Sacraments'. By the end of this session you should know the meaning of 'liturgy', how, when and why it is celebrated, the meaning of a sacrament and the names and classifications of the seven sacraments. Each part will last 25 minutes with 10 further minutes for some summary activities.*

Presentation Part I (25 minutes)

What is the Sacred Liturgy?

Why does the Church have liturgy?

The liturgies of the Church

When is liturgy celebrated?

***The Baptism of Christ* by Piero della Francesca** (c. 1416-1492)

The Baptism of Christ shows a perfect act of worship. The picture's vertical dimension emphasises Jesus as a divine person of the blessed Trinity. The Spirit hovers above him as a dove. The presence of the heavenly Father is indicated by a radiance shining through the overarching tree. The horizontal dimension emphasises Jesus' humanity. Jesus stands as our High Priest in the liturgy and sacraments. We are represented by the catechumen in the background, preparing to follow Christ in Baptism and along the road of discipleship. John the Baptist, on the right, takes the part of the sacred minister in this liturgical act.

Choice of Summary Activities I (10 minutes)

EXAMPLE *You should now know the meaning of 'liturgy'. The following activities should help to reinforce this understanding.*

Summary	Questions to reinforce key points
Discussion questions	Practical activities

The presentation offers the choice of the four optional activities shown on the left. You may select any of these or proceed to part II of the presentation.

Regarding the *'Questions to reinforce key points'*, the hidden answers to the first question, *'What are the key points of the definition of liturgy?'* are:

(1) The true worship of God **(2)** enacted by Jesus Christ and his body, the Church **(3)** through the power of the Holy Spirit **(4)** It is a shared 'public work' (*leitourgia*) **(5)** with ceremonies, rites and formulas **(6)** established by Scripture and Tradition

Conclusion

EXAMPLE *I hope that you feel confident to refer to page 21 of the Participant's Book for the definition of liturgy and for the other subjects we have covered. We now go on to examine the seven sacraments and how they are classified.*

Presentation Part II (25 minutes)

What are the Sacraments?

Why are sacraments important?

What is essential to the sacraments?

What are the effects of the sacraments?

The Communion of the Apostles by Fra Angelico
(c. 1400-1455)

In this picture of the Last Supper, Jesus Christ feeds the apostles one by one with the sacrament of the Eucharist, his own body and blood. In the scene at the centre of the picture Jesus distributes Holy Communion to his beloved disciple John, behind which is the table of the Last Supper. The table resembles the altar at Mass and the room reminds us of the sanctuary of a church. This picture emphasises the centrality of Jesus Christ to all the sacraments and that he is the principal agent acting through his minister in the liturgy today.

Choice of Summary Activities II (10 minutes)

> **EXAMPLE** *At the end of this second part you should be able to classify the seven sacraments according to their liturgical celebration and their effects. You should also have some understanding of why the sacraments are important and how they are administered. The following activities should help to reinforce this understanding.*

Summary	Questions to reinforce key points
Discussion questions	Practical activities

The presentation offers the choice of the four optional activities shown on the left. You may select any of these or proceed to the conclusion.

Regarding the '*Questions to reinforce key points*', the hidden answers to the first question, '*What are the key points of the definition of the sacraments?*' are:

(1) Signs established by Christ
(2) They cause what they signify
(3) They heal us from sin
(4) They plant, nourish or restore God's divine life of grace in us

Conclusion

> **EXAMPLE** *Following this session you should know the meanings of liturgy and the sacraments and how they are celebrated. I also hope you feel confident to refer to pages 21 and 22 of the Participant's Book for a summary of the subjects this presentation has covered. We shall close with the liturgical prayer called the 'Gloria' which we pray every Sunday at Mass.*

> *Glory to God in the highest, and peace to his people on earth. Lord God, heavenly king, almighty God and Father: We worship you, we give you thanks, we praise you for your glory. Lord Jesus Christ, only Son of the Father, Lord God, Lamb of God: You take away the sin of the world; have mercy on us. You are seated at the right hand of the Father; receive our prayer. For you alone are the Holy One, you alone are the Lord, you alone are the Most High, Jesus Christ, with the Holy Spirit, in the glory of God the Father. Amen*

Optional follow-up activities

You may wish to invite the participants to complete one or more of the following activities themselves:

- Read some of the sections of the *Catechism* on liturgy and sacraments, especially the general section on the meaning of liturgy (ccc. 1066-1075) and the general section on sacraments (ccc. 1114-1134).

- Note down their experiences of liturgy in the coming week. It may also be worth encouraging them to prepare or follow-up these experiences by reading carefully through the written texts of these liturgies using a Missal, a Lectionary or the Divine Office.

- Memorize the names of the seven sacraments and the liturgical seasons.

- Read carefully through the words of the Mass in a Missal and think prayerfully about what is being said. You could also invite them to learn some of the key liturgical prayers such as the Gloria or Creed.

Baptism and Confirmation

SACRA MENTS

*e*VANGELIUM

PRESENTER'S GUIDE

Introduction

> **EXAMPLE** *Welcome to our session on 'Baptism and Confirmation'. By the end of this session you should know the meaning and importance of Baptism and Confirmation and how, when and why they are celebrated. Each part will last 25 minutes with 10 further minutes for some summary activities.*

Presentation Part I (25 minutes)

What is Baptism?

Why is Baptism important?

What happens to us through Baptism?

How do we prepare for Baptism?

How Baptism takes place

***The Baptism of St Augustine by St Ambrose* by Benito Gozzoli** (c. 1420-1497)

This picture shows the Baptism of Augustine, a man who had formerly lived an immoral life but who converted to Christianity aided by the prayers of his mother, Monica (who stands behind him). In Augustine's second birth of Baptism, he was cleansed of sin and received grace. He later became a priest, bishop and one of the greatest doctors of the Church. In this picture, Ambrose, a sacred minister, is shown pouring the water over the head of Augustine. Someone holds a white garment on the right to signify the new life of grace. The words on the back wall are said to be those of Ambrose, the 'Te Deum Laudamus' (We praise you O God). Augustine is said to have responded by expressing the faith of his Baptism, 'Te Dominum confitemur' (We acknowledge you to be the Lord).

Choice of Summary Activities I (10 minutes)

> **EXAMPLE** *You should now know the meaning of Baptism and its importance as the gateway to the whole Christian life. The following activities should help to reinforce this understanding.*

Summary	Questions to reinforce key points
Discussion questions	Practical activities

The presentation offers the choice of the four optional activities shown on the left. You may select any of these or proceed to part II of the presentation.

Regarding the '*Questions to reinforce key points*', the hidden answers to the first question, '*What are the effects of Baptism?*' are:

(1) Washes away all sin
(2) Makes us children of God
(3) Makes us members of the Church

Conclusion

> **EXAMPLE** *I hope that you feel confident to refer to page 23 of the Participant's Book for the definition of Baptism and for the other subjects we have covered. We now go on to examine the sacrament of Confirmation.*

Presentation Part II (25 minutes)

What is Confirmation?

Why is Confirmation important?

Confirmation and Pentecost

The seven gifts of the Holy Spirit

How do we receive Confirmation?

Pentecost **by Duccio di Buoninsegna** (c. 1255-1319)

This picture shows the first great event of Confirmation. The whole Church is gathered, represented by Mary and the Apostles together. Mary is at the centre of the scene as the Mother of the Church and the Spouse of the Holy Spirit. The flames of fire on the heads of each of the disciples represent the action of the Spirit on that day of Pentecost. The book represents the message that the apostles are now empowered to preach; the open door symbolises the mission of the Church to the outside world, the good news to be proclaimed without fear.

Choice of Summary Activities II (10 minutes)

EXAMPLE *At the end of this part you should know the meaning of Confirmation. You should also have some understanding of why it is important and what is necessary for its celebration. The following activities should help to reinforce this understanding.*

Summary	Questions to reinforce key points
Discussion questions	Practical activities

The presentation offers the choice of the four optional activities shown on the left. You may select any of these or proceed to the conclusion.

Regarding the '*Questions to reinforce key points*', the hidden answers to the first question, '*What are the seven gifts of the Holy Spirit?*' are:

(1) Wisdom
(2) Understanding
(3) Knowledge
(4) Counsel

(5) Fortitude
(6) Piety
(7) Fear of the Lord

Conclusion

EXAMPLE *Following this session you should know the meaning of Baptism and Confirmation and how they are celebrated. I also hope you feel confident to refer to pages 23 and 24 of the Participant's Book for a summary of the subjects this presentation has covered. We shall close with the beginning of an ancient prayer to the Holy Spirit, 'Veni Creator Spiritus'.*

COME, Holy Spirit, Creator blest,
and in our souls take up Thy rest;
come with Thy grace and heavenly aid
to fill the hearts which Thou hast made.

O comforter, to Thee we cry,
O heavenly gift of God Most High,
O fount of life and fire of love,
and sweet anointing from above.

Thou in Thy sevenfold gifts are known;
Thou, finger of God's hand we own;
Thou, promise of the Father, Thou
Who dost the tongue with power imbue.

Optional follow-up activities

You may wish to invite the participants to complete one or more of the following activities themselves:

- Read some of the *Catechism* on Baptism and Confirmation, especially ccc. 1213-1284 and ccc. 1285-1321.
- Read and pray through the text of the baptismal promises.
- Read and pray through the text of the Confirmation rite.
- Memorize the names of the seven gifts of the Holy Spirit.
- Find, read and pray through one or more of the following passages: Matthew 28:18-20; Acts 1:14; 2:1-47.

The Eucharist

PRESENTER'S GUIDE

Preparation

You may wish to read questions 271-294 of the *Compendium*. You can find additional information in the *Catechism* ccc. 1322-1419 especially: (i) the Eucharist in the economy of salvation (ccc. 1333-1344); (ii) the sacramental sacrifice: thanksgiving, memorial, presence (ccc. 1356-1381); (iii) the paschal banquet (ccc. 1382-1401); (iv) the Eucharist as the pledge of glory to come (ccc. 1402-1405).

Some of the concepts of the Eucharist are quite complicated and a good understanding of the meaning of the term *transubstantiation* is important. This is covered on p. 16 of the *Participant's Book* and ccc. 1386 and ccc. 1413 of the *Catechism*. Since the Eucharist is familiar to many it may be worth sharing personal experiences.

Some practical activities require a Missal.

Introduction

> **EXAMPLE** *Welcome to our session on 'The Eucharist'. By the end of this session you should know the meaning of the Eucharist and how, when and why it is celebrated. You should also understand the central role of the Eucharist in the Christian life and its effects in our lives. Each part will last 25 minutes with 10 further minutes for some summary activities.*

Presentation Part I (25 minutes)

The Eucharist as Sacrifice

Sacrifices in the Old Testament

The Eucharistic sacrifice of Christ

The Seven Sacraments by Rogier van der Weyden (1400-1464)

This picture highlights the intimate association between the offering of the Eucharist and the sacrifice of the Calvary. In the foreground we see the historical enactment of the crucifixion; in the background we notice the priest raising the host at the moment of consecration in Mass. This link shows that Christ's single sacrifice is re-presented on the altars of the Church at every Mass. Weyden places the sacrament of the Eucharist at the centre of the all the other sacraments because it is from this sacrifice of Christ that the power of the other sacraments flow. The Eucharistic sacrifice is the 'source and summit' of the Christian life.

Choice of Summary Activities I (10 minutes)

> **EXAMPLE** *You should now know why the Eucharist is a sacrifice. The following activities should help to reinforce this understanding.*

Summary	Questions to reinforce key points
Discussion questions	Practical activities

The presentation offers the choice of the four optional activities shown on the left. You may select any of these or proceed to part II of the presentation.

Regarding the '*Questions to reinforce key points*', the hidden answers to the first question, '*What is the Eucharist?*' are:

(1) A Sacrifice
(2) A Presence
(3) A Food

Conclusion

> **EXAMPLE** *I hope that you feel confident to refer to page 25 of the Participant's Book for a definition of the Eucharist and, in particular, how it is a sacrifice. We now go on to examine the Eucharist as presence and food.*

Presentation Part II (25 minutes)

The Eucharist as Presence	***The Institution of the Eucharist*** by Joos van Wassenhover (-1480) – *This picture emphasises how Jesus feeds us with his own body and blood. St John stands at the table before the chalice as a priest does at Mass. The jug in the foreground reminds us of the washing of the disciples' feet, showing both Christ's self-giving love and the need for purification from serious sin before consuming the Eucharist. The scene is placed in the apse of a church and the table is appropriately in the position of an altar. Contemporary figures on the upper right show that this event of Holy Communion is for all times and places.*
Is Jesus really present in the Eucharist?	***The Mystic Lamb*** by Jan van Eyck (c. 1395-1441) – *This picture emphasises the connection of the Mass to the eternal liturgy of heaven. Jesus is the Lamb that was slain, the image of Revelation 5:12.*
The Eucharist as Food	

Choice of Summary Activities II (10 minutes)

> EXAMPLE *At the end of this second part you should understand the Eucharist as presence and as food, how we behave towards the Eucharist and the effects of receiving the Eucharist. The following activities should help to reinforce this understanding.*

Summary	Questions to reinforce key points
Discussion questions	Practical activities

The presentation offers the choice of the four optional activities shown on the left. You may select any of these or proceed to the conclusion.

Regarding the '*Questions to reinforce key points*', the hidden answers to the first question, '*What are the effects of receiving the Eucharist?*' are:

(1) Union
(2) Strength
(3) Promise

Conclusion

> EXAMPLE *Following this session you should know the meaning of the Eucharist as sacrifice, presence and food. I also hope you feel confident to refer to pages 25 and 26 of the Participant's Book for a summary of the subjects this presentation has covered. We shall close with a translation by Cardinal Newman of the 'Anima Christi' prayer, often said after Communion.*

> *Soul of Christ, be my sanctification; Body of Christ, be my salvation; Blood of Christ, fill all my veins; Water of Christ's side, wash out my stains; Passion of Christ, my comfort be; O good Jesu, listen to me; In thy wounds I fain would hide; Ne'er to be parted from thy side; Guard me, should the foe assail me; Call me when my life shall fail me; Bid me come to thee above, With thy saints to sing thy love, World without end. Amen.*

Optional follow-up activities

You may wish to invite the participants to complete one or more of the following activities themselves:

- Read some of the sections of the *Catechism* on the Eucharist, especially ccc. 1322-1419.

- Visit a church during the week to pray a few minutes before the Blessed Sacrament. It would especially worthwhile to go when the Blessed Sacrament is exposed for adoration.

- Read carefully through one or more of the texts of the Eucharistic prayers, thinking about what is being said, why it is being said and how it relates to the Eucharist.

- Find, read and pray through one or more of the following passages of Scripture: Matthew 26:26-29; Mark 14:22-25; Luke 22:14-22; Luke 24:28-32; 1 Corinthians 11:23-34; Revelation 7:9-17.

Confession and Anointing

PRESENTER'S GUIDE

Preparation

You may wish to read questions 295-320 of the *Compendium*. You can find additional information in the *Catechism* ccc. 1420-1532, especially: (i) the need for Confession (ccc. 1425-1429); (ii) the conversion of the baptised (ccc. 1427-1429); (iii) the sacrament of Penance and Reconciliation (ccc. 1440-1449); (iv) the Anointing of the Sick (ccc. 1499-1532).

Since those preparing for reception into the Church may find Confession particularly daunting, mentioning some positive personal experience may be of great help to them.

Introduction

EXAMPLE *Welcome to our session on 'Confession and Anointing'. By the end of this session you should know the definitions of Confession and Anointing, why they are necessary and how they are celebrated liturgically.*

Each part will last 25 minutes with 10 further minutes for some summary activities.

Presentation Part I (25 minutes)

What is Confession?

Why is Confession important?

How did Christ establish Confession?

Confession and Reconciliation

What is necessary for Confession?

The Return of the Prodigal Son by Rembrandt (1606-1669)

This picture shows the moment of reconciliation between the father and the son in the parable of the prodigal son (Luke 15:11-32). The son has returned to his father and has confessed his sin; his rags, torn sandals and shaved head in this image represent the condition to which sin has brought him and also his state of penitence. The father has embraced him and welcomes him home with rejoicing. The loving embrace of the father in this image represents the love of God who forgives our many sins with tenderness when we confess them.

Choice of Summary Activities I (10 minutes)

EXAMPLE *You should now know the meaning of Confession. The following activities should help to reinforce this understanding.*

Summary	Questions to reinforce key points
Discussion questions	Practical activities

The presentation offers the choice of the four optional activities shown on the left. You may select any of these or proceed to part II of the presentation.

Regarding the '*Questions to reinforce key points*', the hidden answers to the first question, '*What are the three actions of the penitent in the sacrament of Confession?*' are:

(1) Contrition
(2) Verbal confession of sins
(3) Will to make reparation

Conclusion

EXAMPLE *I hope that you feel confident to refer to page 27 of the Participant's Book for the definition of Confession and for the other subjects we have covered. We now go on to examine the sacrament of Anointing of the Sick.*

Presentation Part II (25 minutes)

What is Anointing of the Sick?

Why is Anointing important?

How did Christ establish Anointing?

What are the effects of Anointing?

How is Anointing given?

The Healing of the Cripple and Raising of Tabatha
by Masolino da Panicale (1400-1447)

This picture of Peter raising the dead woman Tabatha to life (Acts 9:36-42) is not a representation of the sacrament of anointing but it does illustrate certain aspects of the sacrament. The presence of the apostle Peter illustrates the way that Anointing of the Sick is a sacramental action performed by the ministers of the Church, as James 5:13-15 confirms. The picture also underlines the way that Anointing strengthens the life of the soul, sometimes brings bodily healing and is administrated in the hope of the final resurrection of the dead.

Choice of Summary Activities II (10 minutes)

EXAMPLE *At the end of this second part you should know the meaning of 'Anointing of the Sick', why it is important, how it is given and its effects. The following activities should help to reinforce this understanding.*

Summary	Questions to reinforce key points
Discussion questions	Practical activities

The presentation offers the choice of the four optional activities shown on the left. You may select any of these or proceed to the conclusion.

Regarding the '*Questions to reinforce key points*', the hidden answers to the first question, '*What are the effects of the Anointing of the Sick?*' are:

(1) Strengthening of the sick person
(2) Remission of sins
(3) Healing of the body according to God's will

Conclusion

EXAMPLE *Following this session you should know the definitions of Confession and the Anointing of the Sick. I also hope you feel confident to refer to pages 27 and 28 of the Participant's Book for a summary of the subjects this presentation has covered. We shall close with the 'Confiteor', the prayer of penitence we say at the beginning of the Mass.*

I confess to almighty God, and to you, my brothers and sisters, that I have sinned through my own fault in my thoughts and in my words, in what I have done and in what I have failed to do; and I ask blessed Mary, ever Virgin, all the angels and saints, and you, my brothers and sisters, to pray for me to the Lord our God.

Optional follow-up activities

You may wish to invite the participants to complete one or more of the following activities themselves:

- Read some sections from the *Catechism* within the section on the sacraments of healing (ccc. 1420-1532).
- Visit one or more sick persons and pray with them.
- Visit a confessional in a Catholic church and to make a note of what they see there.
- Memorize the 'Confiteor' from a Missal or other prayer book.
- Find, read and pray through the parable of the prodigal son (Luke 15:11-32) and the passage on the Anointing of the Sick (James 5:13-15). Many of the other healings of people by Jesus Christ in the Gospels could also be used, for example the forgiveness and healing of the cripple in Mark 2:1-12.

Marriage and Holy Orders

Preparation

You may wish to read questions 321-350 of the *Compendium*. You can find additional information in the *Catechism* ccc. 1533-1666, especially: (i) the sacrament of Holy orders in the economy of salvation (ccc. 1539-1553); (ii) the three degrees of this sacrament (ccc. 1554-1571); (iii) the effects of this sacrament (ccc. 1581-1589); (iv) Marriage in God's Plan (ccc. 1602-1620); (v) matrimonial consent (ccc. 1625-1637); (vi) the effects of Matrimony (ccc. 1638-1642); (vii) the goods and requirements of conjugal love (ccc. 1643-1654).

Since Marriage itself may be a familiar experience for many it would be good to prepare ways of connecting the participants' own practical familiarity with the concepts in this lesson.

Introduction

EXAMPLE *Welcome to our session on 'Marriage and Holy Orders'. By the end of this session you should know the meaning of Marriage and Holy Orders and how, when and why they are celebrated. Each part will last 25 minutes with 10 further minutes for some summary activities.*

Presentation Part I (25 minutes)

The Sacrament of Marriage

What are the roots of Marriage?

Christ and the sacrament of Marriage

What is necessary for Marriage?

The Marriage at Cana by Giotto di Bondone (1267-1337)

The wedding feast of Cana shows how Christ honours and transforms Marriage. The miracle he worked there, transforming water into wine, is a symbol of the blessing he gives to Marriage and his elevation of this union into a sacrament. The jars in the right foreground, containing the water which will be miraculously turned into wine, are a sign of the New Covenant replacing the Old. The miracle also shows how the sacraments take what is naturally good and elevate them to become instruments of heavenly grace.

Choice of Summary Activities I (10 minutes)

EXAMPLE *You should now know the meaning of Marriage. The following activities should help to reinforce this understanding.*

Summary	Questions to reinforce key points
Discussion questions	Practical activities

The presentation offers the choice of the four optional activities shown on the left. You may select any of these or proceed to part II of the presentation.

Regarding the '*Questions to reinforce key points*', the hidden answers to the first question, '*What does the link between Christ and the Church imply for Marriage itself?*' are:

(1) Joy
(2) Sacrifice
(3) Fruitfulness

Conclusion

EXAMPLE *I hope that you feel confident to refer to page 29 of the Participant's Book for the definition of the sacrament of Marriage and for the other subjects we have covered. We now go on to examine Holy Orders.*

Presentation Part II (25 minutes)

The Sacrament of Holy Orders	*The Ordination of Saint Lawrence* by Fra Angelico (c. 1400-1455)
Where do Holy Orders come from?	*This picture shows the ordination of St Lawrence, one of the most famous deacons of the early Church and a martyr for the faith. The presence of a bishop, priests and deacons in this image illustrates the threefold nature of the sacrament of Holy Orders. The bishop is Pope Sixtus II, also martyred for the faith in the middle of the third century. The chalice, one of the symbols of Holy Orders, is a symbol of sacrifice, which is at the heart of this sacrament.*
How are Holy Orders passed on?	
The call to Holy Orders	

Choice of Summary Activities II (10 minutes)

> **EXAMPLE** *At the end of this second part you should be able to name the three orders of the sacrament of Holy Orders, understand their duties and how this sacrament is given. The following activities should help to reinforce this understanding.*

Summary	Questions to reinforce key points
Discussion questions	Practical activities

The presentation offers the choice of the four optional activities shown on the left. You may select any of these or proceed to the conclusion.

Regarding the '*Questions to reinforce key points*', the hidden answers to the first question, '*What are the three duties of those in Holy Orders?*' are:

(1) To govern
(2) To teach
(3) To sanctify

Conclusion

> **EXAMPLE** *Following this session you should know the meaning of the sacraments of service, namely Marriage and Holy Orders. I also hope you feel confident to refer to pages 29 and 30 of the Participant's Book for a summary of the subjects this presentation has covered. We shall close with the prayer of St Ignatius Loyola, a prayer which applies to all forms of Christian service.*

> *Take Lord, and receive all my liberty, my memory, my understanding, and my entire will – all that I have and call my own. You have given it all to me. To you, Lord, I return it. Everything is yours; do with it what you will. Give me only your love and your grace. That is enough for me.*

Optional follow-up activities

You may wish to invite the participants to complete one or more of the following activities themselves:

- Read some of the sections of the *Catechism* on Marriage and Holy Orders (ccc. 1533-1666).

- Read carefully through the words of the Marriage or Ordination rites, thinking about what happens at each stage of the rite. Note what promises are made and also any references to Scriptural events and persons in connection with these rites.

- Find out the names of the different kinds of vestments that a priest wears during Mass. Suggest that they try to discover what each of these items symbolises.

- Find, read and pray through one or more of the following passages: John 2:1-11 (the miracle at Cana); Ephesians 5:21-6:4 (Marriage and family life); 1 Timothy 4:13-16 (some of the duties of Holy Orders); Revelation 19:6-9 (a vision of the kingdom of heaven with links to both Marriage and Holy Orders).

Moral Action

Preparation

You may wish to read questions 363-376 and 391-400 of the *Compendium*. You can find additional information in the *Catechism*: (i) the spiritual battle (ccc. 407-409); (ii) concupiscence (ccc. 1264); (iii) man's freedom (ccc. 1730-1748); (iv) the morality of human acts (ccc. 1749-1761); (v) conscience (ccc. 1776-1802); (vi) sin (ccc. 1846-1876).

Since the concepts involved in moral action are complex, it would be good to study carefully the first part of the presentation and the definition of moral action at the top of p. 31 of the *Participant's Book*. The second part would be enhanced by adding one or two personal examples of temptations or intimidations.

Introduction

> **EXAMPLE** *Welcome to our session on 'Moral Action'. By the end of this session you should know the meanings of moral action, of sin and the main categories of sin. You should also know how we do what is good and how we contend with the opposition of the world, the flesh and the devil. Each part will last 25 minutes with 10 further minutes for some summary activities.*

Presentation Part I (25 minutes)

What is a Moral Action?	*The Fall and Expulsion from the Garden of Eden* by Michelangelo (1475-1564)

What is sin?

Mortal and venial sin

How can we do what is good?

The picture shows Adam and Eve succumbing to the temptation of the devil and making a free choice that was evil (left). It then depicts one of the catastrophic consequences, namely, the expulsion from paradise (right).

The devil appears in alluring and attractive colours to show how temptation appears under the guise of good. The barren land on the right and the faces of Adam and Eve show some of the consequences of sin.

Choice of Summary Activities I (10 minutes)

> **EXAMPLE** *You should now know what moral action means and how we do what is good. You should also know the meaning of sin and its division into mortal and venial. The following activities should help to reinforce this understanding.*

Summary	Questions to reinforce key points
Discussion questions	Practical activities

The presentation offers the choice of the four optional activities shown on the left. You may select any of these or proceed to part II of the presentation.

Regarding the '*Questions to reinforce key points*', the hidden answers to the first question, '*What are the three conditions of mortal sin?*' are:

(1) Grave matter **(2)** Knowledge
(3) Full consent

The hidden answers to the second question, '*What kind of actions can be sins?*' are:
(1) Thoughts **(2)** Words **(3)** Deeds **(4)** Omissions

Conclusion

> **EXAMPLE** *I hope that you feel confident to refer to page 31 of the Participant's Book for the definition of moral action and the other subjects we have covered. We now go on to examine the battle between good and evil in our own lives.*

Presentation Part II (25 minutes)

Moral Battle and Victory	*The Temptation of Christ* by Duccio di Buoninsegna (c. 1255-1319)
What is the great battle?	*The picture shows Christ's authoritative dismissal of the devil after having been tempted in the desert. The devil is depicted as a fallen angel with darkened wings seductively offering with his right hand all the kingdoms of the world. The world is depicted in all its majestic grandeur and apparent strength: loggias and battlements alternate with bell-towers, roofs and windows, all protected by solid luminous encircling walls. The picture reminds us that Christians also face temptations but have the confidence of victory with the aid of Jesus Christ.*
The world, the flesh and the devil	
The victory of Christ	

Choice of Summary Activities II (10 minutes)

> **EXAMPLE** *At the end of this second part you should be able to name and explain the three opponents to the moral life: the world, the flesh and the devil. You should also have some understanding of how we can be victorious in our struggle with these evil forces. The following activities should help to reinforce this understanding.*

Summary	**Questions to reinforce key points**
Discussion questions	**Practical activities**

The presentation offers the choice of the four optional activities shown on the left. You may select any of these or proceed to the conclusion.

Regarding the '*Questions to reinforce key points*', the hidden answers to the first question, '*What are our opponents in the great moral battle?*' are:

(1) The world
(2) The flesh
(3) The devil

Conclusion

> **EXAMPLE** *Following this session you should know the meaning of moral action, the ways in which we know and achieve what is good, the meaning of sin and the three opposing forces to our moral success. I also hope you feel confident to refer to pages 41 and 42 of the Participant's Book for a summary of the subjects this presentation has covered. We shall close with a prayer to St Michael the Archangel who chose to follow God in humility rather than follow the devil and his rebel angels.*

> *Holy Michael the Archangel, defend us in the day of battle; be our safeguard against the wickedness and snares of the enemy, may God rebuke him, we humbly pray. And do Thou, prince of the heavenly host, by the power of God, cast down to hell Satan, and all evil spirits, who wonder through the world for the ruin of souls. Amen.*

Optional follow-up activities

You may wish to invite the participants to complete one or more of the following activities themselves:

- Read some of the sections of the *Catechism* on moral action, especially on sin (ccc. 1852-1864) and on the morality of human acts (ccc. 1750-1761).

- Make a personal review of how they struggle with the world, the flesh and the devil, reminding them that these struggles take place most frequently in the daily routine of life.

- Learn the Prayer of St Michael.

- Read the account of the temptation and victory of Jesus Christ in Luke 4:1-13 or Matthew 4:1-11. Invite them to read the accounts of Gethsemane in Matthew 26:36-42, Luke 22:39-46 or Mark 14:32-42.

Natural Law and the Ten Commandments

MORALS

EVANGELIUM

Preparation

You may wish to read questions 415-421 and 434-533 of the *Compendium*. You can find additional information in the *Catechism* ccc. 1949-1964 and ccc. 2052-2557, especially: (i) the natural law (ccc. 1954-1960); (ii) the Decalogue (ccc. 2056-2082); (iii) the individual commandments (ccc. 2083-2557).

The second part of the presentation could be enhanced by adding one or two practical examples of ways one can break the commandments in contemporary situations.

Introduction

EXAMPLE *Welcome to our session on 'Natural Law and the Ten Commandments'. By the end of this session you should know the meaning of the natural law and the origin, importance and meaning of the Ten Commandments. Each part will last 25 minutes with 10 further minutes for some summary activities.*

Presentation Part I (25 minutes)

The Natural Law

Natural and civil law

The Ten Commandments

The natural law and the law of grace

Moses by Guido Reni (1575-1642)

This picture shows Moses holding the two tablets of stone with the Ten Commandments carved on them. The clouds in the background symbolise that these commandments have been revealed by God on Mount Sinai. Moses broke these original two tablets in pieces when he discovered that the people had broken God's law (Ex 32:19) by worshipping a golden calf, thereby breaking the first commandment. Later, God told Moses to make copies of the original tablets (Ex 34:1). This may be interpreted as a sign of the indestructibility of the natural law which the Ten Commandments reveal (Rom 2:14-16).

Choice of Summary Activities I (10 minutes)

EXAMPLE *You should now know what natural law means, and its relation to civil law, the Ten Commandments and the law of grace. The following activities should help to reinforce this understanding.*

Summary	Questions to reinforce key points
Discussion questions	Practical activities

The presentation offers the choice of the four optional activities shown on the left. You may select any of these or proceed to part II of the presentation.

Regarding the '*Questions to reinforce key points*', the hidden answers to the first question, '*Why is natural law called 'natural'?*' are:

(1) It is founded on what is good for human nature
(2) It is known by the natural faculty of reason

Conclusion

EXAMPLE *I hope that you feel confident to refer to page 33 of the Participant's Book for the definition of natural law and the other subjects we have covered. We now go on to examine each of the Ten Commandments.*

Presentation Part II (25 minutes)

The Ten Commandments

Commandments regarding God

Commandments regarding others

Commandments regarding desires

This page in the Participant's Book has no picture, but instead has a table of the Ten Commandments with Biblical and modern examples of how these commandments are broken.

Choice of Summary Activities II (10 minutes)

> EXAMPLE *At the end of this second part you should be able to list the Ten Commandments and explain the meaning of each. The following activities should help to reinforce this understanding.*

Summary	Questions to reinforce key points
Discussion questions	Practical activities

The presentation offers the choice of the four optional activities shown on the left. You may select any of these or proceed to the conclusion.

Regarding the '*Questions to reinforce key points*', the hidden answers to the first question, '*What are the main divisions within the Ten Commandments?*' are:

(1) Commandments regarding God (1-3)

(2) Commandments regarding others (4-8)

(3) Commandments regarding desires (9, 10)

Conclusion

> EXAMPLE *Following this session you should know the meaning of the natural law and how it is related to other kinds of law, and also have some understanding of the origin, importance and meaning of the Ten Commandments. I also hope you feel confident to refer to pages 33 and 34 of the Participant's Book for a summary of the subjects this presentation has covered. We shall close with a prayer by St Alphonsus Liguori. This is an act of love and sorrow for sin.*

> *I love you Jesus my love above all things. I repent with my whole heart for having offended you. Never permit me to separate myself from you again. Grant that I may love you always and then do with me what you will. Amen.*

Optional follow-up activities

You may wish to invite the participants to complete one or more of the following activities themselves:

- Read some of the sections of the *Catechism*, especially ccc. 1949-1964 and 2052-2557.

- Make a personal review of how they follow each of the Ten Commandments.

- Review some current news stories in the light of the Ten Commandments.

- Memorize the Ten Commandments.

- Find, read and pray through one or more of the following passages of Scripture: Exodus 20:2-17; Deuteronomy 5:6-21; Matthew 19:16-21.

Grace and the Beatitudes

PRESENTER'S GUIDE

Preparation

You may wish to read questions 358-362; 384-390 and 422-428 of the *Compendium*. You can find additional information in the *Catechism*: (i) the Beatitudes (ccc. 1716-1729); (ii) the theological virtues and gifts of the Holy Spirit (ccc. 1812-1845); (iii) the natural law (ccc. 1965-1687); (iv) justification (ccc. 1987-1995); (v) grace (ccc. 1996-2004); (vi) merit (ccc. 2006-2011).

Grace is difficult to understand because its effects on people's lives go beyond a merely natural conception of human goodness. The best images of the effects of grace are in the lives of the saints, many of whom have lived in ways that are extraordinary in worldly terms; they have not simply been 'good people'. Adding one or two examples from the lives of the saints would enhance the second part of the presentation.

Introduction

> **EXAMPLE** *Welcome to our session on 'Grace and the Beatitudes'. By the end of this session you should know the meaning of grace and how the Beatitudes are blessings that surpass the standards of normal human goodness. Each part will last 25 minutes with 10 further minutes for some summary activities.*

Presentation Part I (25 minutes)

What is Grace?

Traditional terms for the supernatural life

The life of grace

The theological virtues

Mistakes regarding grace

The Baptism of the Neophytes by Masaccio (1401-1428)

This picture shows Peter baptising the new converts to Jesus Christ as recorded in Acts 2:41. The casting off of old garments signifies repentance from a life of sin. The running water signifies the washing away of sin and the 'living water' which Jesus promised (Jn 7:38). The bowl Peter is using is like the bowl that farmers use for scattering seed. This emphasises how the life of grace is like a seed sown in nature, a new life that should be nurtured and bear fruit for an eternal harvest.

Choice of Summary Activities I (10 minutes)

> **EXAMPLE** *You should now know what grace means and how we enter into and grow in the life of grace. The following activities should help to reinforce this understanding.*

Summary	Questions to reinforce key points
Discussion questions	Practical activities

The presentation offers the choice of the four optional activities shown on the left. You may select any of these or proceed to part II of the presentation.

Regarding the '*Questions to reinforce key points*', the hidden answers to the first question, '*What are the different ways that we describe the life of grace?*' are:

(1) Partaking of the divine nature   (3) Being temples of the Holy Spirit
(2) Being co-heirs with Christ   (4) Divinisation

Conclusion

> **EXAMPLE** *I hope that you feel confident to refer to page 35 of the Participant's Book for the definition of grace and the other subjects we have covered. We now go on to examine each of the Beatitudes in turn.*

Presentation Part II (25 minutes)

What are the Beatitudes?

Beatitudes of holy detachment

Beatitudes of holy action and desire

Beatitudes of heavenly living

The Beatitude of persecution for Christ

This page in the Participant's Book has no picture, but instead has a table of the Beatitudes with examples of their application in the Bible.

Choice of Summary Activities II (10 minutes)

EXAMPLE *At the end of this second part you should have some understanding of the names, meanings and main divisions of the Beatitudes and how they surpass natural perfection. The following activities should help to reinforce this understanding.*

Summary	Questions to reinforce key points
Discussion questions	Practical activities

The presentation offers the choice of the four optional activities shown on the left. You may select any of these or proceed to the conclusion.

Regarding the *'Questions to reinforce key points'*, the hidden answers to the first question, *'What eight groups of people are addressed by the Beatitudes?'* are:

(1) The poor in spirit
(2) The mourners
(3) The meek
(4) Those hungry and thirsty for righteousness

(5) The merciful
(6) The pure in heart
(7) The peacemakers
(8) Those persecuted for righteousness' sake

Conclusion

EXAMPLE *Following this session you should know the meaning of grace and the ways in which we gain and nourish the life of grace within us. You should also understand how the Beatitudes are integral to the life of grace. I also hope you feel confident to refer to pages 35 and 36 of the Participant's Book for a summary of the subjects this presentation has covered. We shall close with a prayer which is also an expression and act of charity.*

O my God, I love you above all things with my whole heart and soul because you are all good and worthy of all my love. I love my neighbour as myself for the love of you. I forgive all who have injured me and ask pardon of all whom I have injured. Amen.

Optional follow-up activities

You may wish to invite the participants to complete one or more of the following activities themselves:

- Read some sections of the *Catechism*, especially ccc. 1716-1729, 1812-1835 and 1987-2029.

- Make a personal review of how they can live the Beatitudes in their own lives.

- Learn the Beatitudes.

- Find, read and pray through one or more of the following passages of Scripture: Matthew 5:3-11 on the Beatitudes; Matthew 19:16-30 on the rich young man; Luke 6:20-38 on the Beatitudes and their application; Matthew 5:20-48 on surpassing the goodness of the natural law.

Virtues and Vices

PRESENTER'S GUIDE

Preparation

You may wish to read questions 377-383 of the *Compendium*. You can find additional information in the *Catechism* ccc. 1803-1844, especially (i) cardinal virtues (ccc. 1805-1809); (ii) theological virtues (ccc. 1812-1829).

It is likely that participants will recognise quickly the reality of the virtues and vices when this material is presented. However, some example applications of the virtues and vices to contemporary life may help.

Introduction

EXAMPLE *Welcome to our session on 'Virtues and Vices'. By the end of this session you should know the meaning of virtues and vices and how they are categorised. Each part will last 25 minutes with 10 further minutes for some summary activities.*

Presentation Part I (25 minutes)

What are Virtues?

What are the principal virtues?

How do we achieve the virtues?

The Seven Virtues (details: prudence, justice, temperance, fortitude) **by Giotto di Bondone** (1267-1337)

These images symbolise the four cardinal virtues. The figure at the desk is deliberating and looking in a mirror, emphasising the deliberation and good self-knowledge that prudence requires. The figure with the scales represents the proper rendering of justice to each person. The figure with the armour represents the constancy of fortitude. The figure standing clothed in the doorway, appearing to bind a sword, represents the curbing of the passions through temperance.

Choice of Summary Activities I (10 minutes)

EXAMPLE *You should now know the meaning of the virtues, the names of the cardinal virtues and understand how the virtues are acquired. The following activities should help to reinforce this understanding.*

Summary	Questions to reinforce key points
Discussion questions	Practical activities

The presentation offers the choice of the four optional activities shown on the left. You may select any of these or proceed to part II of the presentation.

Regarding the '*Questions to reinforce key points*', the hidden answers to the first question, '*What are the four cardinal virtues?*' are:

(1) Prudence
(2) Justice
(3) Fortitude
(4) Temperance

Conclusion

EXAMPLE *I hope that you feel confident to refer to page 37 of the Participant's Book for the definition of virtue and the other subjects we have covered. We now go on to examine the problem of vice.*

Presentation Part II (25 minutes)

What are Vices?

The seven deadly vices

The vices and their remedies

The Seven Deadly Sins by Hieronymous Bosch (1450-1516)

This is a series of practical representations of the seven deadly sins, which surround the figure of Christ who forgives and heals sin. The order of the sins, clockwise from the bottom, is: anger, envy, avarice, gluttony, sloth, lust and pride.

At the corners of the picture are the four last things from the session on 'Mary and the Four Last Things'. This shows the connection of the virtues and vices with judgment after death, and how the virtues and vices help to determine what we are to be in eternity.

Choice of Summary Activities II (10 minutes)

EXAMPLE *At the end of this second part you should be able to name and explain the seven deadly vices. You should also have some understanding of how we can counter them with the contrary virtues. The following activities should help to reinforce this understanding.*

Summary	Questions to reinforce key points
Discussion questions	**Practical activities**

The presentation offers the choice of the four optional activities shown on the left. You may select any of these or proceed to the conclusion.

Regarding the '*Questions to reinforce key points*', the hidden answers to the first question, '*What are the seven deadly vices?*' are:

(1) Pride

(2) Envy

(3) Avarice

(4) Anger

(5) Sloth

(6) Gluttony

(7) Lust

Conclusion

EXAMPLE *Following this session you should know what virtues and vices are, the ways in which we can achieve the former and avoid the latter. I also hope you feel confident to refer to pages 37 and 38 of the Participant's Book for a summary of the subjects this presentation has covered. We shall close with a prayer written by St Richard of Chichester.*

Thanks be to you, my Lord Jesus Christ, for all the benefits which you have given me, for all the pains and insults which you have borne for me. Most merciful Redeemer, Friend and Brother, may I know you more clearly, love you more dearly, and follow you more nearly, day by day. Amen.

Optional follow-up activities

You may wish to invite the participants to complete one or more of the following activities themselves:

- Read some of the sections of the *Catechism*, especially ccc. 1803-1829; 1833-1844.

- Make a personal review of how they struggle with the various vices in their lives; invite them to develop the practice of a particular virtue in their lives.

- Learn the names of the four cardinal virtues and the seven deadly vices.

- Find, read and pray through one or more of the following passages of Scripture: Galatians 5:13-26; Ephesians 5:1-5; Colossians 3:1-14.

Christian Life in the World

Preparation

You may wish to read questions 401-414 and 428-433 of the *Compendium*. You can find additional information in the *Catechism*: (i) the human person and the social order (ccc. 1877-1948); (ii) Christian holiness (ccc. 2012-2016); (iii) the precepts of the Church (ccc. 2041-2043); (iv) the family and society (ccc. 2201-2246); (v) life issues (ccc. 2270-2283); (vi) Marriage and chastity (ccc. 2351-2400).

Since this session involves the practical application of Christian teaching to the world today, it would be worth preparing some personal experiences and examples of some of the subjects covered.

Introduction

> **EXAMPLE** *Welcome to our session on 'Christian Life in the World'. By the end of this session you should have an understanding of what is needed to live a good personal and public Christian life. Each part will last 25 minutes with 10 further minutes for some summary activities.*

Presentation Part I (25 minutes)

The Personal Christian Life

Personal prayer life

Personal knowledge

Personal sacramental life

Personal moral life

The precepts of the Church

Christ Carrying His Cross by **Stanley Spencer** (1891-1959)

This is a somewhat abstract representation of Jesus carrying his cross through the suburban streets of an English town. The whole of Cookham High Street has become like the nave of a virtual church, although many of the figures seem indifferent to what is taking place. Carpenters and workmen are associated with Christ in the way that they follow him carrying ladders. The picture represents the way that the Christian life is often lived out in quiet but constant faithfulness amid the business of daily secular life. Beneath the surface of the ordinary can be a miraculous and extra-ordinary Christian reality.

Choice of Summary Activities I (10 minutes)

> **EXAMPLE** *You should now know how to live the personal Christian life in prayer, knowledge, sacraments and moral life. The following activities should help to reinforce this understanding.*

Summary	Questions to reinforce key points
Discussion questions	**Practical activities**

The presentation offers the choice of the four optional activities shown on the left. You may select any of these or proceed to part II of the presentation.

Regarding the '*Questions to reinforce key points*', the hidden answers to the first question, '*What are the six precepts of the Church?*' are:

(1) Attend Mass on Sundays and holy days of obligation
(2) Receive the sacrament of reconciliation at least once a year
(3) Receive holy communion at least once a year during the Easter season
(4) Keep holy the holy days of obligation
(5) Fast and observe abstinence on the prescribed days
(6) Provide for the material needs of the Church

Conclusion

> **EXAMPLE** *I hope that you feel confident to refer to page 39 of the Participant's Book for the meaning of a personal Christian life. We now go on to examine the meaning of a public Christian life.*

Presentation Part II (25 minutes)

The Public Christian Life

Christian society

Vocation

Evangelisation

Acts of charity

Challenging the 'culture of death'

This page in the Participant's Book has no picture, but instead has a table of the seven corporeal and seven spiritual works of mercy.

Choice of Summary Activities II (10 minutes)

> EXAMPLE *At the end of this second part you should understand the main areas of engagement for Christians in their public lives and also the corporeal and spiritual works of mercy. The following activities should help to reinforce this understanding.*

Summary	**Questions to reinforce key points**
Discussion questions	**Practical activities**

The presentation offers the choice of the four optional activities shown on the left. You may select any of these or proceed to the conclusion.

Regarding the '*Questions to reinforce key points*', the hidden answers to the first question, '*What are the seven spiritual works of mercy?*' are:

(1) Convert the sinner

(2) Instruct the ignorant

(3) Counsel the doubtful

(4) Comfort the sorrowful

(5) Bear wrongs patiently

(6) Forgive injustice

(7) Pray for the living and dead

Conclusion

> EXAMPLE *Following this session you should know the meaning of the public Christian life and the challenges that Christians face today. I also hope you feel confident to refer to pages 39 and 40 of the Participant's Book for a summary of the subjects this presentation has covered. We shall close with a prayer of St Francis of Assisi.*

Lord, make me an instrument of Your peace. Where there is hatred, let me sow love; where there is injury, pardon; where there is doubt, faith; where there is despair, hope; where there is darkness, light; and where there is sadness, joy. O, Divine Master, grant that I may not so much seek to be consoled as to console; to be understood as to understand; to be loved as to love; for it is in giving that we receive; it is in pardoning that we are pardoned; and it is in dying that we are born to eternal life.

Optional follow-up activities

You may wish to invite the participants to complete one or more of the following activities themselves:

- Read some of the sections of the *Catechism*, especially ccc. 1877-1948; 2012-2016; 2041-2043; 2201-2246; 2270-2283 and 2351-2400.

- Make a review of the personal and public Christian life applied to their own lives.

- Practise one or more of the spiritual or corporeal works of mercy.

- Learn the precepts of the Church and the corporeal and spiritual works of mercy.

- Find, read and pray through one or more of the following passages of Scripture: Amos 2:6-16; Isaiah 10:1-4; James 2:1-26; Luke 16:19-31 and especially Matthew 25:31-46.

The Life of Prayer

Preparation

You may wish to read questions 534-556, 567-577 of the *Compendium*. You can find additional information in the *Catechism*: (i) what prayer is (ccc. 2559-2565); (ii) prayer in the Bible (ccc. 2566-2622); (iii) prayer in the Church and its Tradition (ccc. 2623-2662); (iv) the way prayer and guides to prayer (ccc. 2663-2696); (v) the life of prayer (ccc. 2697-2724); (vi) the battle of prayer (ccc. 2725-2758).

Since prayer is hard to explain, it would be good to study carefully the parts of the definition of prayer given in the first part of the presentation: this definition is also at the top of page 41 of the *Participant's Book*.

Introduction

> **EXAMPLE** *Welcome to our session on 'The Life of Prayer'. By the end of this session you should know the meaning of 'prayer', its main classifications and the main ways of praying. Each part will last 25 minutes with 10 further minutes for summary activities.*

Presentation Part I (25 minutes)

What is Prayer?

Why do we pray to God?

The principal activities of prayer

Mistaken ideas about prayer

***The Virgin in Prayer* by Sassoferrato** (1609-1689)

This picture has been chosen because Mary's hands are joined in a traditional posture of prayer and because her countenance implies contemplation, one of the forms of prayer. Although her eyes are lowered, if we look up to her she is seen to be gazing upon us, which implies that she is praying for us. Her head is bowed in submission to the will of the Father as the true 'handmaid of the Lord'. The beauty of her countenance reflects her inner loveliness and teaches us that by means of prayer we come to shine with the splendour of God.

Choice of Summary Activities I (10 minutes)

> **EXAMPLE** *You should now know what prayer is. The following activities should help to reinforce this understanding.*

Summary	Questions to reinforce key points
Discussion questions	Practical activities

The presentation offers the choice of the four optional activities shown on the left. You may select any of these or proceed to part II of the presentation.

Regarding the '*Questions to reinforce key points*', the hidden answers to the first question, '*What are the key points of the definition of prayer?*' are:

(1) Thinking of God
(2) Thinking of the things of God
(3) Speaking to God
(4) Listening to God
(5) Desiring to be united with God
(6) Desiring to do God's will

Conclusion

> **EXAMPLE** *I hope that you feel confident to refer to page 41 of the Participant's Book for the definition of prayer and for the other subjects we have covered. We now go on to examine the main classifications of prayer and ways of praying.*

Presentation Part II (25 minutes)

How Do We Pray?

Difficulties in prayer and their remedies

What can help us to pray?

Who can help us to pray?

The Meditative Prayer of St Dominic by Fra Angelico (c. 1400-1455)

This image and others like it were painted by Fra Angelico on the walls of the San Marco convent cells to aid the friars in their prayer. This picture illustrates meditative prayer, one of the four main kinds of prayer. St Dominic is reading Scripture and meditating upon it. The star above his head shows that God is inspiring him: prayer is not simply our own work. The fact that this image is part of a larger fresco called 'The Mocking of Christ' implies that St Dominic is reading about the Passion of Jesus Christ and meditating upon it. This tells us that the events of Scripture are made present to us through prayer.

Choice of Summary Activities II (10 minutes)

> **EXAMPLE** *At the end of this second part you should be able to classify any prayer into one of the four categories of vocal prayer, liturgical prayer, meditative prayer and contemplative prayer. You should also have some understanding of ways of praying, including sources of help for overcoming difficulties in prayer. The following activities should help to reinforce this understanding.*

Summary	Questions to reinforce key points
Discussion questions	Practical activities

The presentation offers the choice of the four optional activities shown on the left. You may select any of these or proceed to the conclusion.

Regarding the '*Questions to reinforce key points*', the hidden answers to the first question, '*What are the main categories of prayer?*' are:

(1) Vocal prayer
(2) Meditative prayer
(3) Liturgical prayer
(4) Contemplative prayer

Conclusion

> **EXAMPLE** *Following this session you should know the meaning of prayer, the main classifications of prayer and the main ways of praying. I also hope you feel confident to refer to pages 41 and 42 of the Participant's Book for a summary of the subjects this presentation has covered. We shall close with a prayer to ask the Holy Spirit to make this knowledge effective in our lives.*

> *Come, O Holy Spirit, fill the Hearts of your faithful, and enkindle in them the fire of your love, send forth your Spirit and they shall be created, and you shall renew the face of the earth.*

Optional follow-up activities

You may wish to invite the participants to complete one or more of the following activities themselves:

- Read some of the sections of the *Catechism* on prayer, especially on the prayer of Jesus (ccc. 2599-2616) and the battle of prayer (ccc. 2725-2758).

- Make a personal review of the role of prayer in their lives, particularly when they pray, what they pray and how long they pray. Invite them to think of ways in which this could be improved.

- Learn one or more of the key traditional Catholic prayers. If they do not already know these, it would be of great value to learn the *Our Father*, the *Hail Mary* and the *Glory Be*.

- Find, read and pray through some key prayers from the Bible, for example: the *Magnificat* in Luke 1:46-55; the *Benedictus* in Luke 1:68-79; the hymn to the humility and glory of Christ in Philippians 2:6-11.

The Lord's Prayer

PRESENTER'S GUIDE

Preparation

You may wish to read questions 578-598 of the *Compendium*. You can find additional information in the *Catechism* ccc. 2759-2865, especially: (i) an introduction to the Lord's Prayer (ccc. 2759-2776); (ii) summary statements about the Lord's Prayer (ccc. 2797-2802); (iii) concluding remarks (ccc. 2857-2865).

It would be helpful to be familiar with the basic structure of the Lord's Prayer; the principal divisions are found in the table towards the top of page 44 of the *Participant's Book*.

Introduction

> EXAMPLE *Welcome to our session on the Lord's prayer. By the end of this session you should know how the Lord's Prayer is structured and what each part of it means. Each part will last 25 minutes with 10 further minutes for some summary activities.*

Presentation Part I (25 minutes)

What is the Lord's Prayer?	**Jesus Taking Leave of the Apostles** by Duccio di Buoninsegna (c. 1255-1319)
The structure of the Lord's Prayer	*This picture shows Jesus teaching his disciples. We know that when they asked him to teach them how to pray he gave them the Lord's Prayer. Notice the veil drawn back on the left hand door which shows that God is revealing himself (revelation means to take the veil back). There is a Marian symbol behind the apostles (a cloth shaped as an M), showing her motherly presence in all Christian gatherings. This garment can also stand for the burial garment of Christ which was left in the tomb after the Resurrection.*
The opening invocation	

Choice of Summary Activities I (10 minutes)

> EXAMPLE *You should now know the origin of the Lord's Prayer, its structure and the meaning of its opening invocation. The following activities should help to reinforce this understanding.*

Summary	**Questions to reinforce key points**
Discussion questions	**Practical activities**

The presentation offers the choice of the four optional activities shown on the left. You may select any of these or proceed to part II of the presentation.

Regarding the '*Questions to reinforce key points*', the hidden answers to the first question, '*What are the three parts of the basic structure of the Lord's Prayer?*' are:

(1) The invocation
(2) The petitions regarding God
(3) The petitions for the good things we need

Conclusion

> EXAMPLE *I hope that you feel confident to refer to page 43 of the Participant's Book for the origin and structure of the Lord's Prayer and the meaning of its opening invocation. We now go on to examine the rest of the Lord's Prayer.*

Presentation Part II (25 minutes)

| What are the Petitions? | *The Agony in the Garden* by Giovanni Bellini (c. 1426-1516) |

What are the Petitions?

Petitions regarding God

Petitions for the good things we need

The Agony in the Garden **by Giovanni Bellini** (c. 1426-1516)

In this picture Jesus kneels in agony prior to his suffering and death. During this prayer, Jesus repeats one of the petitions of the Our Father, "thy will be done" (Mt 26:42). The barren rocky ground, in contrast to the distant greenery, symbolises the lack of consolation that can sometimes be experienced in prayer: An angel is shown coming from heaven to give Jesus strength, which reminds us of how God comes to our aid when we pray. Jesus' disciples sleep in the foreground. With words that recall the penultimate line of the Lord's Prayer, Jesus warns them to pray so as not to enter into temptation (Lk 22:26).

Choice of Summary Activities II (10 minutes)

EXAMPLE *At the end of this second part you should be able to classify and understand the two sets of petitions of the Our Father and how these relate to us. The following activities should help to reinforce this understanding.*

Summary	Questions to reinforce key points
Discussion questions	Practical activities

The presentation offers the choice of the four optional activities shown on the left. You may select any of these or proceed to the conclusion.

Regarding the '*Questions to reinforce key points*', the hidden answers to the first question, '*What are the seven petitions?*' are:

(1) Hallowed be thy name (2) Thy Kingdom come (3) Thy will be done, on earth as it is in heaven (4) Give us this day our daily bread (5) Forgive us our trespasses as we forgive those who trespass against us (6) Lead us not into temptation (7) Deliver us from evil

Conclusion

EXAMPLE *Following this session you should know the origin, meaning and structure of the Lord's prayer and how it is the summary of all Christian prayer. I also hope you feel confident to refer to pages 43 and 44 of the Participant's Book for a summary of the subjects this presentation has covered. We shall close by praying the Lord's Prayer itself.*

Our Father, who art in heaven, hallowed be thy name. Thy kingdom come. Thy will be done on earth, as it is in heaven. Give us this day our daily bread, and forgive us our trespasses as we forgive those who trespass against us, and lead us not into temptation, but deliver us from evil.

Optional follow-up activities

You may wish to invite the participants to complete one or more of the following activities themselves:

- Read some of the sections of the *Catechism* on the Lord's Prayer, especially ccc. 2759-2865.

- Devote some thought and prayer to each of the individual petitions of the Lord's Prayer, covering one petition each day for seven days.

- Learn the Lord's Prayer if they have not already done this.

- As well as the Lord's Prayer (Matthew 6:9-13; Luke 11:2-4), invite them to read and pray through some texts where the same themes can be found in different contexts, for example: Revelation 14:1 (*Our Father, who art in heaven, hallowed by thy name*); Luke 23:42 (*Thy kingdom come*); Luke 1:38 (*Thy will be done on earth, as it is in heaven*); John 6:34-35 (*Give us this day our daily bread*); Mark 11:25 (*and forgive us our trespasses as we forgive those who trespass against us*); Mark 14:38 (*and lead us not into temptation*); Galatians 1:4 (*but deliver us from evil*).

Praying the Mass

PRESENTER'S GUIDE

Preparation

You may wish to read questions 271-294 (on the sacrament of the Eucharist) of the *Compendium*. You can find additional information in the *Catechism* on the liturgical celebration of the Eucharist (ccc. 1345-1355).

Since praying the Mass is something personal as well as public, it may be good to prepare to share some good personal experiences of the Mass. Note that some practical activities require a Missal.

Introduction

> EXAMPLE *Welcome to our session on 'Praying the Mass'. By the end of this session you should know how to pray the Mass well and how to overcome various difficulties. You should also have an understanding of the structure of the Mass. Each part will last 25 minutes with 10 further minutes for some summary activities.*

Presentation Part I (25 minutes)

What is Praying the Mass?

Preparation for Mass

During the Mass

After the Mass

Difficulties with praying the Mass

The Mass and heaven

The Last Supper by Sassetta (1394-1450)

This picture shows the scene of the Last Supper when Jesus celebrated the first Mass with his twelve apostles, offering his life in a ritual sacrifice of bread and wine which became his body and blood. The artist has depicted the table as an altar; the use of the one cup and one bread emphasises the link with the Mass. One apostle does not have a halo. This is Judas, who is present but not really participating in mind and heart. The tree in the distance outside the door has a double significance: it could be the tree on which Judas hung himself or could represent the wood of the cross itself, which is the culmination of the Last Supper.

Choice of Summary Activities I (10 minutes)

> EXAMPLE *You should now know what praying the Mass means and some ways in which our praying of the Mass can be more effective. The following activities should help to reinforce this understanding.*

Summary	Questions to reinforce key points
Discussion questions	Practical activities

The presentation offers the choice of the four optional activities shown on the left. You may select any of these or proceed to part II of the presentation.

Regarding the '*Questions to reinforce key points*', the hidden answers to the first question, '*What is meant by full, conscious and active participation?*' are:

(1) Prayerful engagement
(2) Proper understanding
(3) Good preparation
(4) Application to our lives

Conclusion

> EXAMPLE *I hope that you feel confident to refer to page 45 of the Participant's Book for the definition of praying the Mass and for the other subjects we have covered. We now go on to examine the parts of the Mass.*

Presentation Part II (25 minutes)

The Structure of the Mass

Introductory Rite

Liturgy of the Word

Liturgy of the Eucharist

Communion Rite

Concluding Rite

This page in the Participant's Book has no picture, but instead has a table showing the main parts of the Mass.

Choice of Summary Activities II (10 minutes)

EXAMPLE *At the end of this second part you should be able to list the different parts of the Mass and to explain their significance. The following activities should help to reinforce this understanding.*

Summary	Questions to reinforce key points
Discussion questions	Practical activities

The presentation offers the choice of the four optional activities shown on the left. You may select any of these or proceed to the conclusion.

Regarding the '*Questions to reinforce key points*', the hidden answers to the first question, '*What is the basic five-part structure of the Mass?*' are:

(1) Introductory Rite
(2) Liturgy of the Word
(3) Liturgy of the Eucharist
(4) Communion Rite
(5) Concluding Rite

Conclusion

EXAMPLE *Following this session you should know how to pray the Mass, overcome certain difficulties and engage with its different parts appropriately. I also hope you feel confident to refer to pages 45 and 46 of the Participant's Book for a summary of the subjects this presentation has covered. We shall close with an ancient prayer that refers to the Mass.*

O Sacred Banquet in which Christ is received as food, the memory of His Passion renewed,
the soul is filled with grace and a pledge of the life to come is given us.

Optional follow-up activities

You may wish to invite the participants to complete one or more of the following activities themselves:

- Read some of the sections of the *Catechism* on praying the Mass, especially ccc. 1345-1355.

- Make a personal review of how they pray the Mass. Invite them to think of ways in which this could be improved.

- Attend a Mass during the week, putting the teaching of this session into practice.

- Learn one or more of the key prayers and responses of the Mass.

- Find, read and pray through some of the prayers of the Mass.

The Practice of Confession

PRAYER

*e*VANGELIUM

Preparation

You may wish to read questions 296-312 (the sacrament of Confession) and 434-533 (the Commandments) of the *Compendium*. You can find additional information in the *Catechism* ccc. 1422-1498 and 2052-2557, especially: (i) the acts of the penitent (ccc. 1450-1460); (ii) the effects of the sacrament (ccc. 1468-1470); (iii) the celebration of the sacrament (ccc. 1480-1484).

Those preparing for reception into the Church through this course may find Confession particularly daunting; mentioning some positive personal experience may be of great help to them.

Introduction

EXAMPLE *Welcome to our session on 'The Practice of Confession'. By the end of this session you should know why, how and when we go to Confession and what constitutes a good Confession, including how we prepare by an examination of conscience. Certain difficulties will also be addressed. Each part will last 25 minutes with 10 further minutes for some summary activities.*

Presentation Part I (25 minutes)

The Practice of Confession

When should we go to Confession?

Difficulties about Confession

How do we make a good Confession?

***The Light of the World* by William Holman Hunt** (1827-1910)

This picture has been chosen to illustrate how Jesus visits our souls in Confession bringing his light, love and warmth. Here Christ, who is the light of the world (symbolised by the glowing lantern), knocks at the door of the soul. The overgrowth shows that the door has not been opened in a long time. There is no handle on the outside; it can only be opened from within. This reminds us that God does not force his mercy upon us; we have to open the door of our soul to God. A remarkable fact about this picture is that, while painting it, Holman Hunt experienced a great deepening of his own faith.

Choice of Summary Activities I (10 minutes)

EXAMPLE *You should now know how Confession is practised. The following activities should help to reinforce this understanding.*

Summary	Questions to reinforce key points
Discussion questions	Practical activities

The presentation offers the choice of the four optional activities shown on the left. You may select any of these or proceed to part II of the presentation.

Regarding the '*Questions to reinforce key points*', the hidden answers to the first question, '*What is the sequence of actions in making a Confession?*' are:

(1) Confession of sins

(2) Advice and penance given by the priest

(3) The act of contrition

(4) Absolution

Conclusion

EXAMPLE *I hope that you feel confident to refer to page 47 of the Participant's Book for the definition of what the practice of Confession means. We now go on to look at an examination of conscience which can be used to prepare for Confession.*

Presentation Part II (25 minutes)

| An Examination of Conscience | *This page in the Participant's Book has no picture, but instead has a table showing an examination of conscience based on the Ten Commandments.* |

Sinful actions regarding God

Sinful actions regarding others

Sinful actions regarding desires

The Ten Commandments are a very good way to examine our conscience. Other helpful ways include looking at the seven deadly sins; examining our relationships with God, others and ourselves; looking at sins in thought, word, deed or omission; or simply looking at our lives in the light of God's truth. Whatever way we use, the aim of an examination of conscience is to discover how we have been acting and where we stand in our relationship with God.

Choice of Summary Activities II (10 minutes)

EXAMPLE *At the end of this second part you should know how to make an examination of conscience. The following activities should help to reinforce this understanding.*

Summary	Questions to reinforce key points
Discussion questions	Practical activities

The presentation offers the choice of the four optional activities shown on the left. You may select any of these or proceed to the conclusion.

Regarding the '*Questions to reinforce key points*', the hidden answers to the first question, '*What is needed for a good examination of conscience before Confession?*' are:

(1) A systematic review of my life since my last Confession

(2) My actions seen in the light of God's commandments

(3) The uncovering of any serious matters to which I have knowingly and freely consented

Conclusion

EXAMPLE *Following this session you should know how to practice Confession well and how to make a good examination of conscience. I also hope you feel confident to refer to pages 47 and 48 of the Participant's Book for a summary of the subjects this presentation has covered. We shall close with a simple act of contrition.*

O my God, because you are so good I am very sorry that I have sinned against you, but with the help of your grace, I will not sin again.

Optional follow-up activities

You may wish to invite the participants to complete one or more of the following activities themselves:

* Read some of the sections of the *Catechism* on the practice of Confession, especially ccc. 1422-1498 and 2052-2557.

* Make a personal evaluation of their use of this sacrament.

* Make a personal examination of conscience.

* Learn a simple formula for making a Confession, particularly an act of contrition.

Catholic Devotions

Preparation

You may wish to read questions 351-353, 557-566 of the *Compendium*. You can find additional information in the *Catechism* ccc. 2650-2696 covering (i) the tradition of prayer (ccc. 2650-2662); (ii) the way of prayer (ccc. 2663-2682); (iii) guides for prayer (ccc. 2683-2696).

Since this session refers to many different devotions, it might be helpful to choose a few of the more familiar ones and to show some objects connected with them, for example, a crucifix or icon.

Note that some practical activities require devotional objects, such as a rosary.

Introduction

> EXAMPLE *Welcome to our session on 'Catholic Devotions'. By the end of this session you should know the meaning of a devotion and the main kinds of devotions. Each part will last 25 minutes with 10 further minutes for some summary activities.*

Presentation Part I (25 minutes)

Catholic Devotions (I)

Advent and Christmas devotions

Lent and Easter devotions

Ordinary Time devotions

Devotions to the Holy Eucharist

The Magdalene Reading by Rogier van der Weyden (1400-1464)

This picture shows St Mary Magdalene engaged in prayer using a Book of Hours. This was a traditional medieval devotion with prayers set throughout the day at particular times. The jar of costly oil is a symbol of a devotional act in the Gospels, when the woman took a pound of costly ointment of pure nard and anointed the feet of Jesus and wiped his feet with her hair (Lk 7:36-50). In the background is the symbol of another devotion: a set of rosary beads.

Choice of Summary Activities I (10 minutes)

> EXAMPLE *You should now know what is meant by 'Catholic devotions' and some of the principal devotions of the Eucharist and of the Liturgical Year. The following activities should help to reinforce this understanding.*

Summary	Questions to reinforce key points
Discussion questions	Practical activities

The presentation offers the choice of the four optional activities shown on the left. You may select any of these or proceed to part II of the presentation.

Regarding the '*Questions to reinforce key points*', the hidden answers to the first question, '*What are the key points in the definition of a devotion?*' are:

(1) A customary popular prayer
(2) Often linked to other holy actions
(3) Often linked to holy objects
(4) Often linked to holy places

Conclusion

> EXAMPLE *I hope that you feel confident to refer to page 49 of the Participant's Book for the definition of a devotion and for the other subjects we have covered. We now go on to examine other popular devotions.*

Presentation Part II (25 minutes)

Catholic Devotions (II)

Devotions to the Blessed Virgin Mary

Devotions to the saints and the dead

Shrines and pilgrimages

Recommended devotions for the home

The Wilton Dyptich (late 14th century)

This picture symbolises English Catholic piety at a time when England was renowned for its devotion to Our Lady and was called the 'Dowry of Mary'. King Richard II is depicted on the right with his patrons, St John the Baptist and the English kings St Edward the Confessor and St Edmund of East Anglia, dedicating England to the care of the Mother of God. Mary is surrounded by angels and she is standing on the fruitful earth of the celestial paradise.

Choice of Summary Activities II (10 minutes)

EXAMPLE *At the end of this second part you should know some of the principal devotions to Mary, the saints and the dead, about shrines and pilgrimages and devotions for the home. The following activities should help to reinforce this understanding.*

Summary	Questions to reinforce key points
Discussion questions	Practical activities

The presentation offers the choice of the four optional activities shown on the left. You may select any of these or proceed to the conclusion.

Regarding the '*Questions to reinforce key points*', the hidden answers to the first question, '*What are the four sets of Rosary mysteries?*' are:

(1) Joyful Mysteries

(2) Luminous Mysteries

(3) Sorrowful Mysteries

(4) Glorious Mysteries

Conclusion

EXAMPLE *Following this session you should know about the main kinds of devotions in the life of the Church. I also hope you feel confident to refer to pages 49 and 50 of the Participant's Book for a summary of the subjects this presentation has covered. We shall close with the Angelus prayer which reminds us of the Incarnation, the foundation of all our devotions.*

The angel of the Lord declared unto Mary. And she conceived by the Holy Spirit. Hail Mary…

Behold the handmaid of the Lord. Be it done unto me according to Thy word. Hail Mary…

And the Word was made Flesh. And dwelt among us. Hail Mary…

Pray for us, O holy Mother of God. That we may be made worthy of the promises of Christ.

Let us pray. Pour forth, we beseech Thee, O Lord, Thy grace into our hearts, that we to whom the Incarnation of Christ Thy Son was made known by the message of an angel, may by His Passion and Cross be brought to the glory of His Resurrection. Through the same Christ Our Lord. Amen.

Optional follow-up activities

You may wish to invite the participants to complete one or more of the following activities themselves:

- Read some of the sections of the *Catechism* (ccc. 2650-2696).

- Make a personal review of the devotions used in their homes, local church and families. Invite them to think about what might enrich their devotional lives.

- Find and pray a new devotion.

- Encourage them to learn the words of a simple devotion such as the Rosary.

Catechesis for Non-Catholic Adults (RCIA)

The following suggested sequence of teaching sessions is intended as a systematic education in the Catholic Faith for non-Catholics. It accompanies the three periods of the Rite of Christian Initiation for Adults (RCIA).

Catechesis for Catholic Adults

The following suggested sequence of teaching sessions is intended as a systematic education in the Catholic Faith for those who have already received the sacraments of initiation but who wish to deepen their knowledge and practice.